AF478221

Images of the Downs

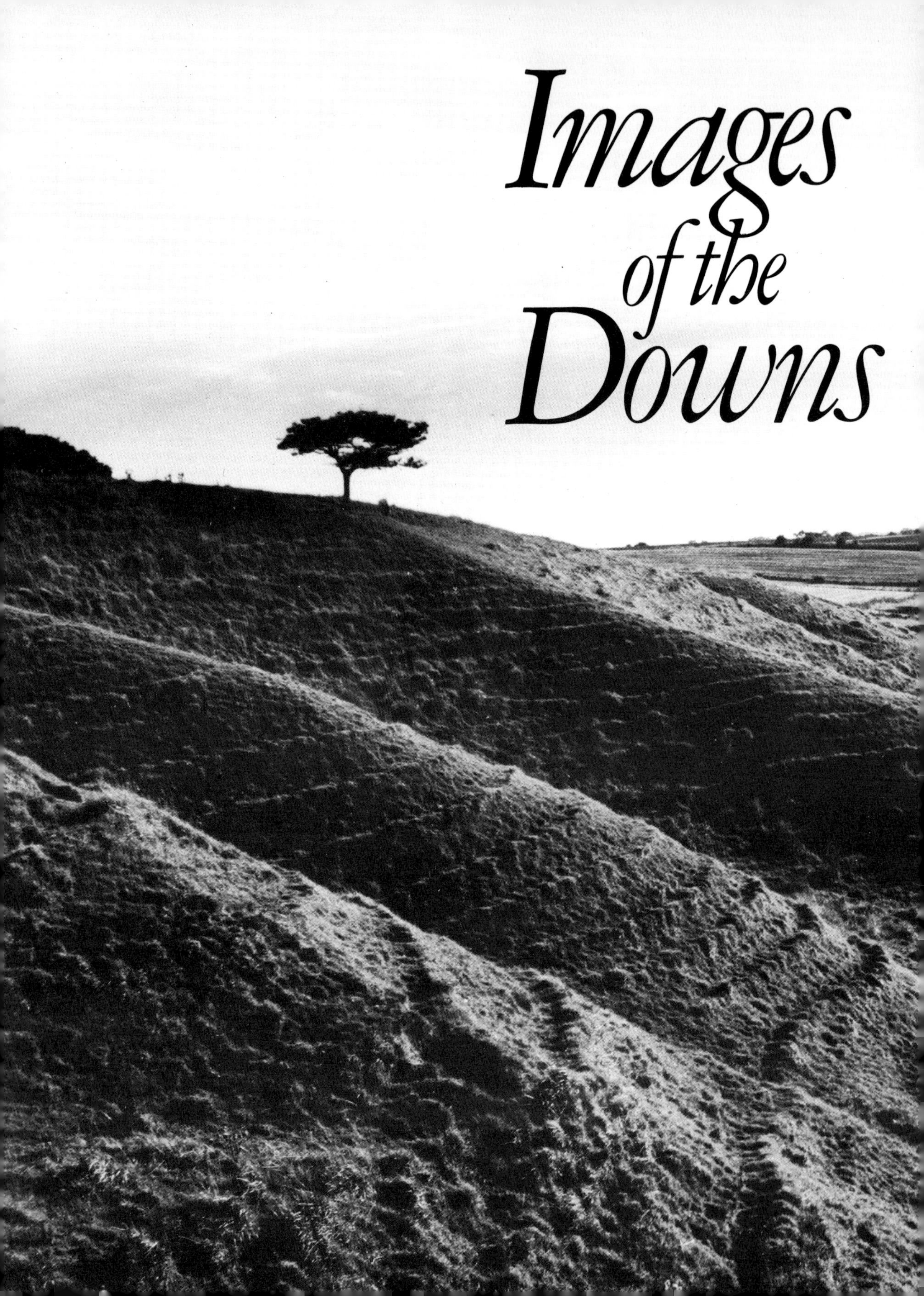

Images
of the
Downs

Photographs by John Mosley · Text by Caroline Hillier

Macmillan London

By Caroline Hillier
The Flood
Dialogue on an Island

By Caroline Hillier and John Mosley
The Western Midlands: A Journey to the Heart of England
The Bulwark Shore: Thanet and the Cinque Ports

Title-page photograph:
The scarp below the Ridgeway, near Wayland's Smithy –
looking towards Liddington Hill

Designed by Robert Updegraff

ISBN 0 333 32469 2

First published 1983 by
Macmillan London Limited
London and Basingstoke

Associated companies in Auckland, Dallas,
Delhi, Dublin, Hong Kong, Johannesburg,
Lagos, Manzini, Melbourne, Nairobi,
New York, Singapore, Tokyo, Washington
and Zaria

Filmset in Palatino by Filmtype Services Limited,
Scarborough, North Yorkshire.

Printed in Hong Kong.

Contents

Acknowledgements

We should like particularly to thank all those people who have allowed photographs to be taken, and who have talked to us about the subject of this book.

For their generous help, we would like to thank *The Society of Sussex Downsmen*; Mr and Mrs Dick Passmore, and Jenny Passmore, of Coombes Farm, Sussex; Mr John Sales, Curator, Bridport Museum; Mr Ted Walker; Mr Laurie Skeats; Mr Douglas Judd; Mr and Mrs Josh Gifford; Mr William Battershell for the most kind loan of books; Julia Quiatkowski of the Greenwood Tree Restaurant, Dorchester; the Gilbert White Museum, for permission to take photographs.

The quotation from 'Estuary', from *Fox on a Barn Door* by Ted Walker, is by kind permission of the author, David Higham Associates Ltd and Jonathan Cape Ltd; the quotation from *The High Path* by Ted Walker is by kind permission of the author, David Higham Associates Ltd and Routledge & Kegan Paul Ltd; quotations from the Goodwood MSS are by kind permission of the Trustees of the Goodwood Estate; the quotations from *The Enigma of Stonehenge* by John Fowles are by kind permission of Anthony Sheil Associates Ltd and Jonathan Cape Ltd; the quotations from 'Ha'nacker Mill' and 'Fragmentary Prelude' from Hilaire Belloc's *Complete Verse* are by kind permission of Gerald Duckworth & Co Ltd.

C.H.
May 1982

For Laura and Willie
For S. H., and for S. A. D.

1

broad backs into the sky . . .

Gilbert White

ATMOSPHERE GEOLOGY AND VISUAL ASPECT

A scenery of the mind's eye, as well as of the eye. A landscape indelible in memory, retraced in dreams, recalled by armchair travellers. A childhood landscape perhaps; one which we recognise, instinctively, and at once.

'Everyone must find their own locality', wrote Richard Jefferies, in *Nature near London*; 'no two persons look at the thing with the same eyes. ... How could I arrange for you next autumn to see the sprays of the horse-chestnut, scarlet from frost, reflected in the dark water of the brook? ... How could I contrive that the cuckoos should circle round the copse, the sunlight glint upon the stream. . . .'

How to find one's own locality? to fill the imagination with scenes perceived with all the senses, not least the sixth. . . . Ultimately there is no substitute for exploration; which is where, in our crowded times, problems arise. The land is not 'ours'; but we can discover it by following the network of footpaths which thread the countryside; pursue our own interests; discover our favourite patch.

There is immense variety on the downs: the bold downs of the Ridgeway; box-covered slopes in Surrey; tree-hung hangers on the western South Downs; pale, low downs in Dorset or the coombs and heights of Cranborne Chase; white cliffs of the Seven Sisters; the great simplicity of Salisbury Plain. But because chalk is an element in all these areas, part of the pleasure of visiting and re-visiting them is that the traveller finds features of downland in whichever part he may be; he will re-find the known lines and composite details, seen in a new, and yet the same, guise. He has to a supreme degree the freshness of discovery with the nostalgia of coming home. Chalk is a primeval landscape, *the* primeval landscape of southern England, unchanged in large areas, having its great continuity

Scarp of the South Downs from Truleigh Hill

9

with the past; not overlaid too much with later soil, rising unadulterated and uncloying and supremely simple – and, where we have allowed it, unspoilt – from the surrounding regions.

'Why is it', the novelist John Galsworthy asked, 'that in some places one has such a feeling of life being, not merely a long picture-show for human eyes, but a single . . . growing thing, of which we are no more important a part than the swallows and magpies, the . . . sheep in the meadows . . . the winds? . . . In these rare spots . . . one is conscious of an enwrapping web or mist of spirit . . . of all the vanished shapes once dwelling there. . . .'[1]

Nowhere in England is one more conscious of the vanished shapes once dwelling there, than on the chalk downs. Not only the scenery of the mind's eye for so many people who have known them, but also a place where we become aware, half-consciously, of a collective past – somewhere between myth and fact, and truer than either – felt in our bones, and with every sense. The broad backs of the downs, sunny short turf of tumuli and barrows, fast-moving cloud shadows; fluting song of the skylark, scent of crushed thyme; fallen sarsen rocks, dewponds; tracks older than the species of tree around them and strange coruscations from the first farmers, the first ceremonies; brittle skeletons of small animals, trodden underfoot; fixed in the chalk, fossils of sea-creatures older than the landscape. On the downs you are not only half-way to the sky, whatever that may hold for you of ethereality, but bombarded by all the sensations of the earth, and of the layers under the earth, and the seasons; and swept clean by the wind. Always, or usually, the wind: exhilarating, refreshing, inspiring, sometimes awesome.

> *Then the hills of the horizon –*
> *That is how I should make hills had I to show*
> *One who would never see them what hills were like.*
>
> *. . .*
>
> *There were other things*
> *Real, too . . .*
>
> *. . .*
>
> *My past and the past of the world were in the wind.*[2]

'. . . everything is older than we think,' W. G. Hoskins has written.[3]

'Never heard of it – and I've lived here seventy years,' said an old inhabitant, of Whitehawk Neolithic Camp, over which he daily walks his dog.

'The only relics you'll find is us,' said three gardeners in their allotments there. 'The only excavating is what we do . . . the banks and ditches are made by motorbikes.'

Covered in part by the pulling-up ground of Brighton racecourse, weighed down by pre-war semis and flats, with its sunny but often vandalised allotments and sheds, its flotsam of old mattresses, tin cans,

litter, scoured by motorcycles and the wind, Whitehawk Camp is still matchless for its (urbanised) views to the other hills of the area – to Cissbury and Chanctonbury and the downs rolling inland, powerful on the skyline, towards the interior, forming the dark cliffs of the sea of the Weald. A good starting point, for the Sussex hills.

Whether exploring the downs with the help of Ordnance Survey maps – or without maps, as did the poet Edward Thomas – 'I have used good maps in my time, largely to avoid the towns; but I confess that I prefer to do without them and to go . . . guided by the hills or the sun or a stream'[4] (a map, is however, essential for tracing footpaths) – or whether enjoying at a distance or in recollection one of the many facets of downland, it is helpful to know something of their underlying structure.

Fontmell Down, Dorset

The chalk layers were laid down from about 100 million to 65 million years ago, in the period during which dinosaurs became extinct, before the age of mammals, birds and flowering plants. During this Cretaceous period the sea extended over most of Britain (and at one time over 80 per cent of the earth's surface) – a warm sea containing sponges and reptiles. (Chalk is a consolidated oceanic ooze, almost pure calcium carbonate in places – as at Newhaven – composed mainly, it is now believed, from the debris of coccoliths (part of plankton), which sink to the seabed when they die. Scattered in the chalk are fossils of many kinds, including those of fishes, sea-urchins, sea-lilies, ammonites and sponges.)

In one of the periods of great uplift and folding, which had also helped shape the layers of rock beneath, the chalk rose from the sea, in the west exposing new land, with new rivers draining from west to east. In the south-east, the high Wealden area rose. Compression from the south – the same compression that pushed up the Alps – created short, offset folds in a sheaf from the east of the Weald to the borders of the West Country. As the Weald rose, rivers flowed down its flanks, and others south across the Hampshire basin. The centre of the Weald (a geological unit which surprisingly reaches in one direction to northern France) was eroded by sea, weather and rivers, washing flints down into the adjoining areas, leaving the chalk rims of the North and South Downs on either side of the vanished cap. New seas, new deposits followed – sea sand is found at such places as Headley Heath near Box Hill; receding water left sharp terraced scarps on one side of many downs, contrasting with gentler dipslopes. New rivers were cut; the thawing of frozen land at the time of the last Ice Age left dry valleys, or coombs.

Fold on fold, sea on sea, wave upon wave of erosion, river upon river. It is hardly surprising that the downs have the moving, flowing quality of a land ocean, the linear quality that is their essential beauty.

Salisbury Plain was, and is, the central node of the chalk downs, of the chalk (once two thirds of England) that was not eroded at an early date, or overlaid with fresh deposits. From it, outcrops run eastwards to the Hampshire Downs, to the North and South Downs; westwards to the Z-shaped Dorset Downs; north-eastwards, to the Marlborough Downs, to the magnificent scarps of the White Horse Downs (I adopt J. R. L. Anderson's terminology for these Berkshire/Oxfordshire downs; 'We're fighting to get them back,' they will say in Berkshire), and – beyond the scope of this book – on up to West Norfolk, and to the Lincolnshire and Yorkshire Wolds, with an extremity at Flamborough Head. The Isle of Wight, which was at one time part of the southern bank of the Solent, continuing the line of the Frome, has chalk ridges which correspond to the North and South Downs, on either side of an eroded Weald-like cap. At the southern tip of the island, with St Boniface Down, the ridge is less extensive than to the north, where it runs from the Needles to Culver Cliff.

. . . they are the most spacious plaines in Europe, and the greatest remaines that I can heare of of the smooth primitive world when it lay all under water. . . .

. . . And, to speake from the very bottome of my heart . . . methinkes he is much more happy . . . that at ease contemplates the universe as his own, and in it the sunn and starrs, the pleasing meadows, shades, groves, green banks, stately trees, flowing springs, and the wanton windings of a river . . . than he that with fire and sword disturbs the world, and measures his possessions by the wast that lies about him.[5]

> *Ah! what a life were this! how sweet! how lovely!*
> *Gives not the hawthorn bush a sweeter shade*
> *To shepherds, looking on their silly sheep,*
> *Than doth a rich embroider'd canopy —*[6]

John Aubrey, and Shakespeare. How much more it applies in our day.

Downland grasses

Information is not everything. Somehow we have to crack the problem of conserving our countryside and having access to it, on foot, sometimes alone, and certainly for long enough to absorb the different rhythms, atmosphere of a place, to be surprised by animals and birds rather than surprising them. Ordinary pleasures. The first swallow of summer; crows and a mistle-thrush feeding in ploughland; finches noisy in flowering hawthorn. Surrounded by a smell of rabbit and snake, fresh earth, among sheets of milkwort and vetch, Germander speedwell, dustings of grass, skipper butterflies. In our eagerness to inform ourselves we might fall into the trap deplored by John Fowles in his book *The Enigma of Stonehenge*:

> Today is crowds, cars, coaches, lavatories, shops. . . . All skeleton, no heart. We can never regain the old landscape or the emotional effect of the old monument, just as a wild animal in a zoo can never

14

effectively resemble the wild animal in its natural habitat. Only a very few now, the fortunate archaeologist, the fortunate photographer, can hope to have a glimpse of it. The rest of us must stay as imprisoned, as rejected, as the stones themselves; and like them, can only stand and wait for better days.[7]

Or fight for those better days. And meanwhile, one can visit Stonehenge in midwinter, walk on the downs at sunset, or after rain, revisit well-trodden paths until they become new.

Where could we get a good view of Eggardon? I asked someone who lives in Dorset within sight of that hill. (Eggardon can often have the over-green aspect of a postcard view.) He suddenly remembered that from the top corner of a certain field, when hoeing on winter evenings in the past, the great hill, and smaller Shipton Hill, by his own land, had taken on aspects of grandeur. 'They were inspiring, awe-inspiring then.' Showing their hard edge, looming darker, as we found them to be from that angle.

While quietly searching for something else, you will see new aspects of countryside: a roe deer may hover at the edge of a wood, or leap through corn – a different experience to the day-long wait behind a high-powered telescope.

Even the best-known downland sites have a prevailing power. On a hot summer day I watched couples, in sandals or on insecure heels, with or without noisy teenagers or children in pushchairs, climb up the massive ramparts of Maiden Castle in Dorset. This conglomerate earthwork spreading over one hundred acres straddles two hills. Its central plateau appears large enough to contain the whole of adjoining Dorchester with its modern outskirts. On it you can still get lost, find yourself in a maze of trenches up to 60 feet deep, the grass circles rearing skywards. The view is indescribably vast.

Each couple, as they came down from the site, seemed refreshed, held hands, as if they had been relieved for a while of the tensions of twentieth-century civilisation.

———◇———

. . . with great hills as pictures hung on a wall to gaze at. (Richard Jefferies)

Writers who have pinpointed the qualities of downland – in whatever age they wrote, and with whatever degree of practicality or passion – have highlighted its essential elements in their different ways.

Gilbert White, on the 'chain of majestic mountains' of the South Downs: 'As you pass along, you command a noble view of the wild, or weald, on one hand, and the broad downs and sea on the other . . . somewhat analagous to growth in their gentle swellings and smooth fungus-like protuberances, their fluted sides, and regular hollows and slopes . . . so made to swell and heave their broad backs into the sky. . . .'[8]

John Burroughs, an American, in 1883: 'The South Downs form a very remarkable feature of this part of England, and are totally unlike any other landscape I ever saw. I believe it is Huxley who applies to them the epithet of *muttony*, which they certainly deserve, for they are like the backs of immense sheep, smooth, and round, and fat. . . .'[9]

Richard Jefferies: 'On the slope here the furze is flecked with golden spots, and the black-headed stonechats perch on ant-hills or stray flints. . . . Afar, blue line upon blue line of down is drawn along in slow curves, and beneath, the distant sea appears a dim plain with five bright streaks, where the sunshine pours through. . . . The wind is wide, and blows not only here, but along the whole range of hills. . . .'[10]

W. H. Hudson: 'the illusion of infinite distance', 'they stand naked to the sky, and on them the mind becomes more aerial.' [11]

H. J. Massingham: 'star-gazing shoulders', 'islanded in the past'.[12]

Edmund Blunden: 'huge images of creative calm'.

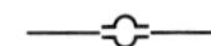

'Older than the centuries'[13] – but the downs and their archaeology were surprisingly unknown in comparatively recent ages.

Sunday, 7 January 1649. A bitter winter. Three weeks before the execution of Charles I.

> . . . I never saw the country round Marlborough till Christmas 1648, being then invited to Lord Francis Seymour. . . . The morrow after twelfth day Mr Charles Seymour and Sir William Button of Tokeham, baronet, met with their pack of hounds at the Grey Wethers. These downs look as if they were sown with great Stones, very thick, and in a dusky evening they look like a flock of Sheep. . . . Twas here our game began and the chase led us through the village of Avebury: where I was wonderfully surprised at the sight of those vast stones. . . . I observed in the enclosure some segments of rude circles made with these stones whence I concluded they had been of old times complete. I left my company awhile, entertaining myself with a more delightful indagation: and then (steered by the cry of the hounds) I overtook the company and went with them to Kennet where was a good hunting dinner provided.

John Aubrey, whose *Monumenta Britannica*[14] was written at the command of Charles II. Our first great English field worker and archaeologist, one can only be thankful that, aged 22, he found archaeological investigation 'a more delightful indagation' than hunting. And this in an age when, as he himself wrote in the Preface to his *Natural History of Wiltshire*, one of the earliest area books, 'Till about the yeare 1649, 'twas held a strange presumption for a man to attempt an innovation in learning. . . . Twas held a sinne to make a scrutinie into the waies of nature. . . .'

Aubrey took a plan, 'donne by memorie alone' to Court, as Charles II, on hearing that Aubrey considered Avebury 'did as much excell Stoneheng, as a Cathedral does a Parish church', was intrigued (Charles having himself seen Stonehenge when fleeing after the Battle of Worcester). Charles made a digression to see Avebury on his way to Bath a fortnight later, with Aubrey as his guide. The King also rode to the top of Silbury Hill (the largest man-made hill in Europe). Aubrey obeyed his command to write a description of ancient remains, barrows and earthworks. The book was never finished, and waited long to be published. Known perhaps best for his *Brief Lives*, Aubrey died in poverty. He is buried somewhere in the church of St Mary Magdalen in Oxford: 'John Aubery A stranger was Buryed Jun 7th' (1697). He had requested: 'on the southe downe of the farme of Broad Chalke [which had been his], on the top of the plaine, is a little barrow (not very high) called by the name of Gawen's Barrow. ... I was never so sacralegious as to disturbe, or rob his urne, let his Ashes rest in peace: but I have often times wish't that my Corps might be interr'd by it.'

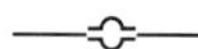

And today? When Stonehenge is roped off to prevent tourists harming the stones, and traffic hurries through the village of Avebury?

It would be inconceivable to be disappointed by either place.

Approaching Avebury, by chance at night, striking into the Marlborough Downs with on the right, the Celtic Oldbury Camp, a Roman road and the Saxon-era Wansdyke starting at Morgan's Hill; on the left, Cherhill, where Mesolithic hunters settled about eight thousand years ago – none of this visible in the moonless, mist-filled darkness, but only the rise of the ground, the thin rows of trees tapering black against a black skyline. (The earthwork lies in a hollow of the downs.) A tightening of the neck muscles, prickling of the scalp, approaching the electricity-filled enigma and powerful storehouse of the past that is Avebury. An outer circle of ninety-eight stones within a ditch and bank, the latter a little over 1 km in circumference; two inner circles, with few remaining stones; originally two avenue approaches; part of the village lying within the site. The huge stones reached at this time of night along a silent road, lit by car headlights, their rough facets gleaming, appearing from nowhere, crashing up out of fog-filled fields and hedges. By day they are just as powerful but more earthly.

Nothing seems to dispel more vigorously any theories of extra-terrestrial visitors, than their place and fittingness in the landscape. Dragged from where they were scattered over the downs at the end of the last Ice Age, the great sarsens (Saracen stones) echo the shapes of the land; hollows and incisions on their sides are gaunt as the bare branches of an ash tree in winter; encrustations of bluish or ochre lichens mottle the rocks. Rocks which belong with the rooks and sheep and grassy mounds; with the rain and mist and pale sunlight. Early lambs in spring huddle against their flanks for shelter; a blackbird is blown on to a crag; a black-faced ewe-lamb uncurls from a cavity hole. A total harmony reflecting what H. J. Massingham called 'the monumental simplicity' of Wiltshire. In this context, the oldest church (and the one at Avebury is not new), the most medieval of houses, look modern, superimposed on the landscape; our present-day features, such as factory blocks and towers, even those country ones of Wiltshire, jar and obtrude.

It is not that the stones or the landscape have not changed – both have altered since the sarsens were placed there: it is the rightness of the choice of site, of material used, the superb endeavour in creating something both child-like and magnificent. The place must have been not only religious, but peaceful in purpose. Looking at Avebury, one is aware of the impulse that every child shows when it picks up pebbles on a beach, and arranges them in patterns in the sand with a thumb; or heaps up sand in ridges, to try to keep back the oncoming tide. Avebury; our urge to create; our defence against the tide. We have come a long way since those simple thumb-marks on the landscape, but cannot yet equal them.

The avenue of stones called the Kennet Avenue snakes its serpentine way to the Avebury ring from the south, across the present road and fields (short straight lengths making up the zig-zag curves). The avenue is a good place to appreciate the balance and packing-in of the stones. The great Swindon Stone, which overhangs the road, weighs about 60 tons. (In 1938, a man's skeleton, that of a zealous helper in destruction of the circles in the Middle Ages perhaps, was found trapped between a stone and the edge of its pit, his barber surgeon's tools beside him.)[15]

Looking back down the stones of the Kennet Avenue, one is struck by the aspects of the sarsens, which stand like strange prophets staring towards Avebury. Illusion upon illusion; another element of a place so full of symbols that it gnaws at memories of which we can never now be certain, but which are part of us and our history.

> *The Druid's groves are gone – so much the better:*
> *Stone-henge is not – but what the devil is it?*[16]

Byron's response to the old stones is more spirited than John Aubrey's.

Now roped off, Stonehenge still rises, despite tea-counter, lavatories and windblown guardians in plastic shelters (all more discreetly unevident than some guidebooks would have you believe), stark and powerful on the expanse of Salisbury Plain. There is nothing like Stonehenge, the supreme monument of the downs. The most finished stone circle in Europe, much smaller in circumference but more advanced and precise than Avebury, with more sophisticated material in the Welsh bluestones used in part, it rises like the least insubstantial of dreams in the centre of a milky range of

The Kennet Avenue,
Avebury

downs in mist, or on the bare plain, in sun. Clumps of trees divide on the skyline, echoing the divisions between the great stone doorways, glimpse upon glimpse of space, into infinity. Geometry, astronomy, ceremony: a shout of triumphant creativity.

Crows fly silently across with heavy wings. 'It hums', as Tess of the d'Urbervilles said to Angel Clare. 'The wind, playing upon the edifice, produced a booming tune, like the note of some gigantic, one-stringed harp.' A line of chalky plough epitomises downland. In the field, a beech-filled hollow. High above, a skylark sings dizzily, in that dichotomy of the megaliths – is its song more, or less, piercing than the poetry of the sarsens? It is certainly part of it. Skylarks *are* downland, are part of Stonehenge.

19

... suddenly a lark starts into the light and pours forth a rain of
unwearied notes overhead. With bright light, and sunshine, and
sunrise, and blue skies the bird is so associated in the mind, that even
to see him in the frosty days of winter, at least assures us that
summer will certainly return. ... High above, the songs of the larks
fall as rain – receive it with open hands.[17]

Round barrows lie near the henge – one can be seen through the stones,
on the down beyond. The inspiration of the builders of the round barrows
was to place them just below the brow of a down, so that they appeared to
the onlooker below to be on the skyline. The sides of the stones at
Stonehenge are very smooth, in close pairs like thighs, softened by
pernod-green or ochre or grey-white lichen. The lintels are firmly bedded,
heavy and yet aerial. Fallen stones lie abandoned in the grass. Farther off,
cows are placid. But there is nothing homely about Stonehenge, and in
spite of the streams of traffic, you approach it almost with fear, certainly
with a sense of heightened awareness.

Who built it? Who were the successive peoples of the downs? Why did
they choose these sites? (For twenty centuries the chalk was the principle
home of prehistoric man, living above the lower forest and swamp lands.)

—◦—

21

The history of downland is linked to the changing climate, and water-table, which was much higher in prehistoric times, but varied even then. After the Ice Ages, with intervening periods of a tundra-like vegetation where primitive hunters used rough flint weapons, came the melting of the glaciers, and birch and pine woods, with shrubs such as juniper and willow – an all-enveloping growth, above which hilltop tracks alone made travel possible. About nine thousand years ago the climate suddenly changed, with long spells of dry, warmer weather, during which hazel and pine spread, and elm and oak appeared. This was followed by an Atlantic phase, with temperatures warmer than ours, and a damper climate, in which oak and elm flourished, with some lime and alder. The land bridge between Britain and the Continent was inundated, making Britain an island.

Mesolithic or Middle Stone Age hunters, who had stone tools, and dogs for hunting, were followed by Neolithic or New Stone Age people, who lived in a more settled way, and were the first farmers, bringing with them across Europe knowledge of crop cultivation, and the use of domestic animals such as sheep, cattle, goats and pigs. Because the water-table was high, they could settle in the drier parts of the country, on the chalk uplands, which they cleared of trees. (The water-table is the surface below which fissures and pores in the strata are saturated with water, and lies between the upper damp layers and the saturated layers. Chalk being porous, rain easily sinks into the ground, accumulating above the lower, impervious strata. The water-table fluctuates, affecting streams, rivers and wells. Modern aerial photography and recent excavations have also shown evidence of lowland settlement, in many areas of the country, but the evidence is buried under our modern villages and ploughland, so that it is in the chalk hills that the patterns of early civilisation will always, for the layman, be most strikingly evident.)

The Neolithic peoples were the people of causewayed camps, long barrows, simple henges and flint mines. That the weather was much wetter when the mines were worked than at present is suggested by the finding there of snail shells of a wet-climate type. The following Bronze Age corresponded with another change in climate, to colder and drier weather. Water supplies became scarcer on the chalk, and settlements came down lower into the valleys under the chalk escarpments. Beech and hornbeam were introduced into the south-east, beech dominating in some areas. The transition from the Neolithic to the Bronze Age, around 2600 BC, nearly five thousand years ago, was the age when Avebury was built, and was followed by the era of the final stages of Stonehenge, of the great Wessex culture – the age of round barrows, splendid gold torcs, bronze tools, trade and population growth. When the climate changed once more, to moister and cooler summers, farmers of the Iron Age cultivated the chalk uplands, using a scratch plough in little rectangular fields. This was the age of hill-forts and, some have thought, of the first dewponds.

New invasions followed, of Celts and Belgae, and finally of the Romans, who still cultivated the chalk uplands, the South Downs being almost totally cleared of vegetation, for instance, and arable cultivation there probably reaching a high level that it has not since exceeded. It was not until the Saxons that settlements were finally concentrated at the foot of the hills, where they efficiently cleared the lowland forest, and obtained water from the springs at the foot of the scarps. (Some streams were intermittent. A winterbourne is a spring of water, as found in chalk districts, which flows only during or after a wet season. Many place names are preceded by 'Winterbourne'.)

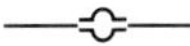

Chalk retains moisture well, and cool breezes blow over the downs, so where not too steep, they provide good land for cultivation. You can sometimes find flowers on the hills when a valley wetland may be parched dry.

After the high downs were cleared of forest growth, the cropping of sheep, and of the rabbits which were introduced by the Normans, kept down undergrowth.

Slonk Hill, South Downs

Trees, especially beeches (and lately conifers), have been replanted, but in essence the landscape of the downs goes back a very long way. Few people have lived on the high downs since the Roman age. But Salisbury Plain, the centre of the chalkland, was once a metropolis. Central Wiltshire shows more evidence of prehistoric occupations over a long period than anywhere else in England. Parts of Sussex provided flint mines for early peoples – as it were, one of our first industrial zones. (Later, also along the Sussex downland and coastal strip, there was a great granary and market-garden area for the Roman legions, exporting to the Continent.) The routes linking these places, and running outwards from Salisbury Plain, were some of the earliest tracks of our ancestors. The past is, on all sides, visible on the downs.

But not everywhere.

In about 1800, there was a furze-covered hillock, alive with rabbit burrows, in Hove, in what was known as Coney-burrow Field. Every Good Friday young people played 'Kiss in the Ring' and other games there. (As was the custom on Palm Sunday and Good Friday, on hills and prehistoric earthworks, probably since pre-Christian times, since the times of the Spring Festival of the Saxon goddess Eostre.) 'Hey diddle-derry, Let's dance on the Bury', was a traditional chant.

1856. A road was cut through Coney-burrow Field to the Brighton-Portsmouth railway. Labourers removed earth from the mound, and in the centre found a rough coffin between 6 and 7 feet long, hollowed out of a tree trunk, which when exposed to the air immediately crumbled, leaving only a few knots of the oak wood. There were small fragments of bone, the head of an ironstone axe-hammer, a small whetstone and a bronze dagger or spearhead. Also a dark red amber cup, with a handle on the side, ornamented with a band of fine lines. It is all but unique, one of our greatest archaeological treasures – a prized possession in Brighton Museum and Art Gallery. (A fragment only of another cup was found near Maiden Castle.) Amber, like pearls and jet, was valued from very early times. It was held to be sacred to the great mother-goddess; amber beads were placed in barrows to help the dead on their last journey; charms were worn to protect the eyes and to ward off the ague.

The mound was reckoned to be at least two thousand if not three thousand years old, and the grave goods indicated a pre-Roman chieftain (the cup is now dated to *c.*1500 BC – Early to Middle Bronze Age). A local antiquarian recounted at the time of the discovery: 'The last clod of that earth which so long covered the bones of a British chieftain was this afternoon carted away; and coffin, bones and earth have been thrown pell-mell to form the mould of the future rosary of Palmyra square.'[18]

1694. One Walter Stretch smashed up a stone from the outer ring at

Avebury, obtaining twenty cartloads of pieces for the Catherine Wheel Inn. *1701.* Some of the avenue stones were taken for a bridge over the Winterbourne. *1706.* Another stone was being used as a fish-stall on market days. Between 1711 and 1719, a farmer Green broke up stone after stone for his farm at Beckhampton. (During the religious zeal of the early Middle Ages, many of these heathen stones had already been toppled into pits and covered with rubble by eager villagers.) When the antiquarian Stukeley visited Avebury first in 1719 it was a wreck. Stones were taken for walls, barns, churches and houses – with the result that many houses at Avebury today have damp walls where lumps of sarsen stone resist modern damp courses.

Retribution was sometimes sharp. An excavation of Silbury Hill in 1849 was followed by a terrible thunderstorm which '. . . made the hills re-echo to the crashing peals, and Silbury itself, as the men asserted who were working at its centre, to tremble to its base.'[19]

Today, depredation is more quietly insidious. Between 1954 and 1964, according to quoted figures, in Wiltshire alone 250 out of a total of 640 scheduled ancient monuments were destroyed or badly damaged. Bronze Age barrows and other monuments in the Isle of Wight have been more recently ploughed up.[20]

1982. A Brighton bypass is proposed by the Department of Transport. The land needed for this, with link roads, would include about 200 acres of agricultural land, and 90 acres of open land, and would cut into the fringes of the downs, creating great and lasting damage to the downland land-scape. In particular it would cut through Southwick Hill, owned inalien-ably by the National Trust, who at a Public Inquiry have pointed out its value as chalk downland. Its atmosphere of peace and quiet, providing a variety of habitats for birds, plants and butterflies (including the chalk-hill blue), and the views of and from the hill, are at risk, as are the old beech trees in Stanmer Woods, farther along the route. A Celtic trackway and a field system would be affected.

'How many bypasses are needed in this country?' was pertinently asked at the inquiry. (It has been pointed out that relief to the town centre with this bypass would be questionable.)

'It would open up the downs', is a seemingly benevolent opinion I have heard voiced. To 'open up' the downs, with dual carriageways, picnic-spots, and carparks, is to destroy them, to negate their inspiring character.

A national loss we cannot afford.

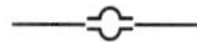

Before the ages of religious zeal (and motorway madness), the Romans had respected ancient sites, and had re-fortified old hill forts (as at Cissbury Ring in Sussex, the second largest earthwork in the country). They built temples within other enclosures, but left places such as Avebury un-

touched. They probably travelled out from their towns of Cunetio (Marlborough), and Durocornovium (Wanborough), to visit the stone circles – a visitor's bronze brooch of a date soon after the AD 43 invasion was found there, and Roman coins have been found in wells in the neighbourhood, perhaps dropped in by superstitious Romano-British locals.

The fortifications of the late Roman era, against marauding Saxons, were followed, after the withdrawal from Britain of the legions, by the years of Saxon invasion and settlement, at the foot of the downs; by the last stand of the legendary Arthur, at Mount Badon (the location of which is uncertain – certainly a hilltop not too far from Avebury); by further cycles of unrest, warfare and invasion, down to the short-lived peace achieved by King Alfred with the Vikings, and King Cnut's championship of a united England. The Norman invasion saw the start of a new order of society and of the great parks and royal forests of the Middle Ages. Where the downs and surrounding area were not given over to sheep walks, they were likely to be hunting preserves, reserved for the king and subject to harsh forest laws. Names such as Kingswood, Buckland, Hartswood and Prince's Coverts in Surrey, Tollard Royal, King's Stag, in Wiltshire and Dorset, have clear origins.

In the fourteenth century, the Black Death in its successive outbreaks killed from one third to one half of the population of the country, and with the decline in labour for arable land and an increase in sheep grazing, many of the remaining inhabitants of settlements were driven out to make way for sheep. The downs had taken on their lonely aspect which in some parts they would never again lose.

But the travellers to the sites of ancient habitations, of ancient ceremonies, and to the rolling green hills 'as pictures hung on a wall to gaze at',[21] hills amongst which Englishmen increasingly took their sport, had only just begun.

The first detailed account of a foreigner's impressions of the type of life led by Englishmen in their remoter countryside, as early as 1466, remarked on the rich game in royal parks, such as that around Salisbury, where they saw hosts of fallow deer, hares and rabbits (but no wolves). They also described vast flocks of sheep, snow white with a few black ones among them.[22]

Taine, in his *Notes sur l'Angleterre,* referring to 'wild, abandoned common lands ... the primitive soil' of England, quotes a sixteenth-century traveller, who remarked: 'Among the English, the nobility regard it beneath them to live in towns; they live in the countryside ... devoting themselves to country pursuits, selling their wool and cattle'.

Another, German, traveller, of the seventeenth century, again remarked on the sheep: 'the sheep are as big as calves in Germany, and they too are left to graze at night, since there are no wolves in England.'[23]

By the late eighteenth century, there was a peak of enthusiasm for travel in England, by both foreigners and Englishmen. A Russian, Nikolai Karamzin, writing home: 'What a country! Everywhere green meadows with great herds of cattle ... everywhere fine country houses, surrounded by parks and lakes, and, as far as the eye can see, coaches, carriages and horsemen, hurrying up and down from London. ...'[24]

By 1787, Johann Wilhelm von Archenholz was writing, 'The English are certainly the greatest walkers in all Europe.'[25]

The downs, where Englishmen could enjoy their passion for walking and riding to the full, were their ideal scenery. And, for the more historically minded traveller, offered images of the past. Emerson, the American essayist and poet, wrote of the English, 'They are good lovers, good haters, slow but obstinate admirers, and, in all things, very much steeped in their temperament, like men hardly awaked from deep sleep, which they enjoy. *Their habits and instincts cleave to nature.* They are of the earth, earthy; and of the sea. ... They are full of coarse strength, rude exercise, butcher's meat, and sound sleep.' He describes a visit to Stonehenge:

It looked as if the wide margin given in this crowded isle to this primeval temple were accorded by the veneration of the British race to the old egg out of which all their ecclesiastical structures and history had preceded . . . this simplest of all simple structures . . . had long outstood all later churches, and all history, and were like what is most permanent on the face of the planet: these, and the barrows. . . . Within the enclosure, grew buttercups, nettles, and, all around, wild thyme . . . and the carpeting grass. . . . At the inn, there was only milk for one cup of tea. When we called for more, the girl brought us three drops. . . . My friend was annoyed who stood for the credit of an English inn, and still more, the next morning, by the dog-cart, sole procurable vehicle. . . .[26]

Of a later downland edifice, Arundel, Johanna Schopenhauer had written: 'alone, under the shadow of ancient trees, these mighty reminders of past grandeur are the finest England has to offer of the kind, rich as the country is in monuments of the past. . . . We left by a route along the shore; a gentle wind barely ruffled the moonlit surface of the water . . . the waves rustled and whispered . . . we travelled without mishap to Brighton.'[27]

The downs were, and are, accessible. Old coach roads may have been rutted and mired, but to the walker, the man on a horse, the summit of the downs could be quickly reached, the plateaux wandered over.

On the downs, you can be, as in few other places in England, away from it all – not only away from the bustle of everyday life, but in tune with the serenity of the landscape. It is still true, as Richard Jefferies wrote, nearly a century ago, in 1885, that 'On a summer's day Wolstanbury Hill is an island in sunshine; you may lie on the grassy rampart . . . alone, among the butterflies and humming bees at the thyme, alone and isolated. . . . Many go to the Dyke, but none to Wolstanbury Hill.'[28] Like him you can look down on the trees far below – 'Where there are beech trees the land is always beautiful; beech trees at the foot of this hill, beech trees at Arundel in that lovely park . . . beech trees in Marlborough forest. . . . Beech and beautiful scenery go together.' On a bank holiday weekend you can be alone on Wolstonbury Hill with perhaps one other walker, climbing up past the moss-covered roots of beeches, past tangles of wild roses and traveller's joy, past the erect wayfaring trees and wind-blown hawthorn, to the grassy summit over whose rim you walk as over the edge of the known world, to see the blue Weald below in a smoke of evening light, trees whitened by evening sun. Cows tread out their lynchets round the steep hillside; small birds soar and dive; the grasses studded with cowslips or orchids, salad burnet or sweet vernal grass, send up their warmth, and down where the buds of beeches fall in a magenta backdrop behind the first leaves and the white pillar of a whitebeam – the Saxon's white tree or beam – the sudden outpouring of a nightingale's song transcends time, and space, with its eloquent otherworldliness.

But stay on the summit, close to the green ramparts, the dewpond, the 'rich blue of the unattainable flower of the sky'. Stay while the sun goes down, while time rolls back, while a 'thousand many stranded grasses' claim your attention as they did that of Goethe's young Werther, watching his valley darken and the last rays of the sun steal into the thickets, feeling 'the world and the sky come to rest within' him.

For there is, as Richard Jefferies said, 'a dust which settles on the heart as well as that which falls on a ledge.'[29]

On the downs the wind sweeps clean the ledges of the mind.

Beech branches –
Wolstonbury Hill

2

. . . Cliffs Rocks Deeps Shallows . . .

John Keats

If the downs were only grass, the story would soon be told: one would agree with Aubrey, on Salisbury Plain – 'The turfe is of a short sweet grasse, good for the sheep, and delightful to the eye, for its smoothnesse like a bowling green, and pleasant to the traveller; who wants here only variety of objects to make his journey less tedious. . . .' But it is natural to the downs to have spectacular features which break up the sameness;[1] in parts lapped by the sea; in others cut through by the clearest of rivers; in almost all areas made dramatic by the clefts and contours of dry coombs. It is this sudden juxtaposition of peaceful idyll and startling elemental edge that brings you up short, makes you disbelieving of the tameness of the downs, as sometimes portrayed in watercolours or over-complaisant verse. There is no need to stand on Shakespeare Cliff at Dover to feel on the 'dread summit of this chalky bourn'.[2] Looking down into the dizzying bowl of coomb and valley from high points in Cranborne Chase or of the White Horse Downs, gives a new perspective on space, and intimation of the rugged core underlying grass and crops, as muscles of a wild animal lie under its pelt. It is practical to take a stick when scaling up and down some of the coomb sides, where furze and sheep alone are sure of a foothold.

The sea gives colour to the downs. 'Green Sussex fading into blue, with one gray glimpse of sea', as Tennyson immortalised it.[3] It adds another dimension to some of the most beautiful downland settings, not only in Sussex, but in Dorset also. The curves of the Seven Sisters, the sparkling Channel with its little boats or slowly turning ships seen from Lancing or Seaford Head, is matched by the grandeur of downland seascapes such as that from Black Down in Dorset (which always does look black; on its summit a monument to Vice-Admiral Sir Thomas Masterman Hardy, Flag

The River Wylye

Captain to Nelson at Trafalgar) across westwards to the strangely flat-topped Golden Cap where the chalk has worn away, shining golden in a setting sun, against a silver sea. Or from Black Down to the east, the cliffs which from inland seem to rear seawards, and at the coast can be white and sharp, as at White Nothe, dropping into the bluest of seas, from downland that is all soft mounds and yellow grass, ringed with lynchets, brooched with barrows and sewn with marguerites and buttercups. The names themselves of these areas seem to sing of the sea: Chaldon Herring and Hambury Tout, Burning Cliff and Shipton Hill, Ringstead Bay and Thorncombe Beacon, Bridport, Seatown and Fleet. Their derivation may in some instances be other, but they seem as apposite as Sussex's Shoreham and Newhaven, Seaford and Beacon Hill, Saltdean and Beachy Head (said to be derived from *Beau Chef*, not from 'beach').

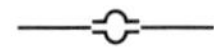

> *No one feels so deeply as the Englishman the irrepressible,*
> *seductive call of the horizon.*
> (Kazantzakis)[4]

Into the sea flow the estuaries, wide and lazy or deep between downs. Traps for sunsets and mists, rime; skyscapes that make fitting finales to downland operas, tatters of flame and glory incandescent between the dark hills.

As Swinburne describes it: '. . . Shoreham, crowned with the grace of years; Shoreham, clad in the sunset. . .'[5]; or Ted Walker:

> *As the image of the sun*
> *after the blinding moment*
> *lasts on the closed lids violet*
> *an instant . . .*

in the inlet of the estuary, where

> *they picked the purple winkles*
> *like scatterings of damsons*
> *with salt dried like bloom on them.*[6]

Not much winkle-gathering along these coasts now. The oyster smacks have left Shoreham; the Brighton 'Juggs' or seashore inhabitants no longer carry their fish along the Juggs Road, a downland path to Lewes, to market their catch there. (The art of fishing is said to have been brought to Sussex by St Wilfrid, who landed in 680, at Selsey, to find a heathen South Saxon population dying from thirst and famine after a three-year drought, some even so desperate that they preferred to drown themselves in the sea. He taught them – who had previously only been able to catch eels in ponds – how to fish with nets, and won his first converts. During the baptism, the rains at last fell. His cathedral and monastery lie beneath the sea; fishermen used to speak of hearing the muffled sounds of a bell under the

The River Adur at Shoreham

water when the wind was still, and of fishing in 'the Park', which was a deer park until Henry VIII's day.)

Local boats do still go out; there are local fish, crab and lobster in south coast shops; fresh, because they haven't travelled to market. 'It's a way of life,' a fisherman said recently. A way of life increasingly under pressure. With boats costing up to £20–30,000 to buy and equip; the pressure from foreign boats, so that local fishermen find themselves 'on the tail end' of whatever's going.

Nets, if no longer dried on the Steine in Brighton, are still made at Bridport (a traditional centre for nets, lines, twines and cordage – the streets were made wide so that each house in the past could have a 'ropewalk'); hand-braiding is still carried out at Loders and Uploders in the area, and (aircraft) nets made in homes at Puncknowle.

At Shoreham-by-Sea a flint-walled sail- or net-store survives – precariously, because not listed – on a riverside site known as Ropetackle.

The industries of sea and rivers were a counterpart to the agricultural industries and other means of livelihood on the downs, the earliest industrial enterprise being that of flint mining.

Flint is the oldest industrial mineral in the world. Found to a large extent in the upper chalk as nodules or 'tabular' tile-like sheets, it was probably formed as a silica gel, which would explain the many fossil impressions found in it. The nodules come in all sizes and shapes, round balls or long fingers, doughnut-shaped or hollow with small flints inside. Small flints with holes used to be threaded on a string and hung on a door, bed-post or round the neck as a talisman against witches, and were known as 'hag-stones'; or hung on a horse's collar to ward off disease; or called 'lucky stones' by children.[7]

There is no certainty as to how the flint bands were formed. A vast number consist of silica dissolved in the Chalk Sea millions of years ago, much of the silica being secreted as sponge spicules (the minute stiffeners which keep a sponge in shape as whalebones do a corset). But silica is also laid down in chalk in other ways. Flints within flints are found, and some flints are still being formed.

Clay-with-flints occurs where on level land flints and clay from marly bands were left, the deposits accumulating in places – capping hills for instance, where trees such as beeches can grow, as at Chanctonbury Ring in Sussex, or Cherhill Down in Wiltshire, or along much of the top of the wooded North Downs.

Fossils are, literally, anything which is dug up, but in the usual sense, the mineralised remains of organisms such as bones, shells, plants, or their impressions or trace. Some fossils are the internal casts of shells; other shells are preserved with flint both inside and outside them; others are coloured patterns in flint, showing the shape of a creature.[8] Sea-urchin fossils can have common names such as 'shepherd's crown', 'fairy loaf', 'pixy helmet' or 'fairy heart' – they were amulets to ensure food, or protection, or love.

> *Wonderful is this wall of stone, wrecked by fate*
> *The city buildings crumble, the bold works of the giants decay. . . .*[9]

Flint is hard, durable, can scratch glass, outlasts granite and the mortar of walls. Ancient flint knives are still razor-sharp. The old axe-heads have been used to fell trees; old hand-axes, the first, Palaeolithic, handle-less axes, fit comfortably into the palm. Flint was a vital part of man's economy for at least half a million years.

The flint mines of Neolithic times can be traced by the pitted surface of downland grass. There were mines at Cissbury, Harrow Hill north-west of Worthing, Findon, Blackpatch and Stoke Down, and at Easton Down in Wiltshire (farther north, at Grime's Graves in Norfolk). Large round pits up to 50 feet deep were dug, with galleries running from them. Crude lamps were used – black sooty patches have been found on walls; picks and wedges were made from deer antlers; bone and stone tools were used. At about the time of Abraham, 2000 BC, the industry was flourishing, with flint for tools, weapons and ritual articles being carried along the ancient ridge-top trackways to the great centres such as Stonehenge. Chippings and flakes of flints can be picked up on the downs; older hammer-stones are found, and flint 'pot-boilers', the stones used by Stone Age man to heat his water, by dropping them red-hot into the water pot, which might have been a mammoth skull.

At Cissbury, the buried skeleton of a girl was found, under the fallen roof of a gallery, the charred remains of a torch in her hand; and the body of a young man was surrounded by chalk blocks in a bare grave. As in so many instances, past deaths prove less elusive than the lives people led. It is difficult to imagine the Neolithic flint-miners at their work; perhaps less difficult to imagine a man in 3000 BC using the large axe-polishing stone found near Ford in Sussex, now in Worthing Museum, or to recreate in one's mind the fashioning of a Late Bronze Age cauldron of overlapping metal pieces riveted together, housed in the same museum. (Flint was still being mined in the Bronze Age, but the manufacture of bronze, and the emergence of the great Wessex culture, brought an era of rich metal-working, trade and craftwork – which, in Sussex also, fused with local tradition.) An admirable gold bracelet found on the beach between Bognor and Selsey; gold torcs and ornamentation; bronze urns and weapons; beads and beakers; loom weights found on a farmstead, bring the era closer to us. While some finds of the later, Roman and Romano-Celtic period – vases and bowls, enamelled gold brooches and pendants, enamelled cheek-pieces for a horse's bit, coins and mosaics – have an enviable quality and sophistication.

The Romans, besides adapting old hill-forts (already more in number by the Iron Age, with new ones built and ancient hilltop meeting places and causewayed camps fortified), chose prime sites on or near the downs for their villas. They had ports, as at the head of Radipole Lake (Weymouth), Noviomagus (Chichester) and Portus Adurni, besides their inland head-quarters. (Portus Adurni was probably at Portchester, although early historians tended to link it with the Adur River, siting the port at Bramber or Aldrington.)

It was the Saxons who made the river valleys their own. The change in climate, perhaps, the lowering of the water-table through drainage, and the more thorough clearance of forest in the low-lying areas with their better tools, enabled them to exploit the belt of deep soils below the scarps, and for water they turned to the springs which gushed so freely at the scarp-foot.

He sendeth Springs
Into the valleys
Which run among the hills.
Oh that men would
Praise the Lord
For his goodness.

At Fulking at the foot of the South Downs, one of these springs, originating by Devil's Dyke, gushes out as a clear stream along the underhill road. Its ornate little pumphouse, which is said to have been put up at the instigation of John Ruskin, to improve the water supply, bears the above inscription. (Ruskin had a friend in Brighton, John Willett, and visited Fulking to admire the sunsets.) Sheep-washing used to be done in the brook. Now, it lines the road, bordered by rush and flags and brooklime, in the village which present-day inhabitants have garlanded with clematis.

The Ruskin spring at Fulking, below the South Downs

Brooks, streams, rivers. In Surrey, the Mole, burrowing under Box Hill, and the Wey, cut through the North Downs on their way to the Thames. The Stour, Medway and Darent cut gaps in Kent. From the Hampshire Downs, streams and rivers drain north or south. In Sussex, the South Downs are cleft by the Arun, Adur, Ouse and Cuckmere rivers, each with its own character, each with its ribbon of Saxon settlements. Down the Adur, Steyning, which had a Saxon mint, probably the site of the original harbour on the Adur (later removed to Old then to New Shoreham and now to Portslade), Bramber, Beeding, Botolphs with its still existing tall narrow church, Old Shoreham with another ancient church. Down the Ouse in its wide meandering course – once filling the whole valley with waters in which herring and porpoise abounded – Lewes, which had two mints; Iford, Rodmell, Southease, Pidinghoe. Along the scarp, other settlements – Edburton, Poynings, Clayton – and in dry valleys, yet others such as Jevington. The *ing* names of the coast, as Lancing, Sompting; the *hams* of the valleys, and the upland *tons*. Bosham, where Cnut's young daughter lies buried, and where he tried to defy the waves; East Dean, where King Alfred had a residence (at Steyning is the one-time grave of his father); Arundel, which was only a small settlement then, now magnificently castled beside the Arun, whose valley has its most rare reaches at Amberley. There, the Wild Brooks, a mingling of brook, pool and dyke among reeds and pastureland, opulent with rare plants and overflown by wildfowl, become at floodtime a gleaming mirage which prompted Freya Stark to write, 'I have never seen any country more exquisite than these Sussex downs'.[10]

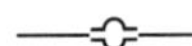

If there is more exquisite country it must be that of the Wylye valley.

> There are other chalk streams in Wiltshire and Hampshire and Dorset – swift crystal currents that play all summer long with the floating poa grass fast held in their pebbly beds, flowing through smooth downs, with small ancient churches in their green villages, and pretty thatched cottages smothered in flowers – which yet do not produce the same effect as the Wylye. Not Avon for all its beauty, nor Itchen, nor Test. Wherein, then, does the 'Wylye bourne' differ from these others, and what is its special attraction? . . . What I discovered was that the various elements of interest, all of which may be found in other chalk-stream valleys, are here concentrated, or comprised in a limited space, and seen together produce a combined effect on the mind. . . .[11]

So W. H. Hudson sums it up, in *A Shepherd's Life*.

Between high downs, through country which Cobbett called 'singularly bright and beautiful', adding, 'It is impossible for the eyes of man to be fixed on a finer country',[12] the Wylye flows with the clarity peculiar to chalk streams (filtered through chalk uplands and then breaking out to flow over hard, clean riverbeds) and with their swift, but not too swift current. Willows and aspens fringe the water. Dog-roses 30 feet high climb the trees; the hillsides flower with spice-scented agrimony (once used for cold cures), scabious and marguerites, while comfrey down by the water droops its 'ivory-white and dim purple blossoms'.[13] In the Wylye, river crowfoot streams like green hair, its daisy-like flowers in champagne-bubbles below the surface, over which pied wagtails scutter and dive. Black-and-white cows wander; a bare-backed angler sits impassive among rushes – a still from a French film; traffic from the A36 is out of sight of the narrow road along the opposite bank. At Steeple Langford, with its weir and pools, a short curved lead cap of steeple emerges from trees; the water swirls and eddies under the weir; time stands still. At Hanging Langford are black-and-white cottages chequered with flint and stone; at Wylye many thatched roofs; at Stockton, red-and-white chequerwork and stone and half-timber; at Heytesbury, the impressive Heytesbury House, on a site where Henry II's mother, the Empress Maud, is said to have had a palace. Twenty villages or hamlets, where the Saxons settled, within 18 miles between Warminster and Wilton, each one seeming more pleasant than the last. In spring, floods swim between the rain-washed downs (even when winter floods have not been severe); rooks' nests ride in the trees; bare willows reflect in water. The soft, light-filled texture of the English countryside, which as Hudson said of Constable's portrayal of Salisbury spire under a rainbow – 'I am informed by artists with the brush, only a madman would undertake, however great a genius he might be.' Salisbury, once known as 'the Sink of the Plain', with its spire, than which Hudson found 'nothing in the architecture of England more beautiful'.[14]

Converging on Salisbury, the other rivers of the plain. The Avon, beswanned at Upavon and Enford, bechurched at Netheravon and Fighel-dean, with gunfire from the army ranges startling the birds from the water-meadows where ancient willow trunks rise gnarled like a lost species. For, as A. G. Bradley observed, early this century, in *Rivers and Streams of England*, 'times have changed on the banks of the Avon. ... Netheravon ... is now the quarters of colonels and majors. At any moment, too, you may meet on the uplifted highway above the stream a group of cavalry scouts, watching for a distant glimpse of imaginary Teutonic invaders, or a train of military waggons rumbling northwards. ... Every one knows that the Crown has recently purchased a portion of Salisbury Plain for the better prosecution of military manoeuvres. ... Sometimes the whole course of the little river from Salisbury to its source is proclaimed by the makers of the great war game to be the coast of England. ...'[15] Although tanks, not cavalry, are now likely to sweep you into the verge as you cross the plain, and more sinisterly, to the east, Porton Down presupposes other war games. Places such as Imber, H. J. Massingham's perfect downland village, are out of bounds, half destroyed, visited for rare church services by those who once lived there.

The Nadder and Ebble, flowing also through villages, the Nadder to Wilton, the Ebble through Broad Chalke, where were the winter town houses of the farmers of Cranborne Chase, and where John Aubrey lived and was church warden. Then the River Bourne with its Winterbournes, and the chalk rivers of other areas. The Kennet, more scrub-fringed than the Avon but ennobled by history. (At Ramsbury – a village like Chilton Foliat, loosely strung out along the chalk valley with space between generous slopes for its houses – Saxon bishops had their seat; at Marl-borough there was the finest coaching hostelry in England, on the site of a medieval castle. The tall beeches of Savernake Forest near by were once a royal forest.)

And all the clear, small rivers of Dorset, such as the Allen, Brit, Piddle and Winterborne, not to mention the Stour, and the Frome, Hardy's Froom of the Valley of the Great Dairies.

The River Tarrant at Tarrant Rawston

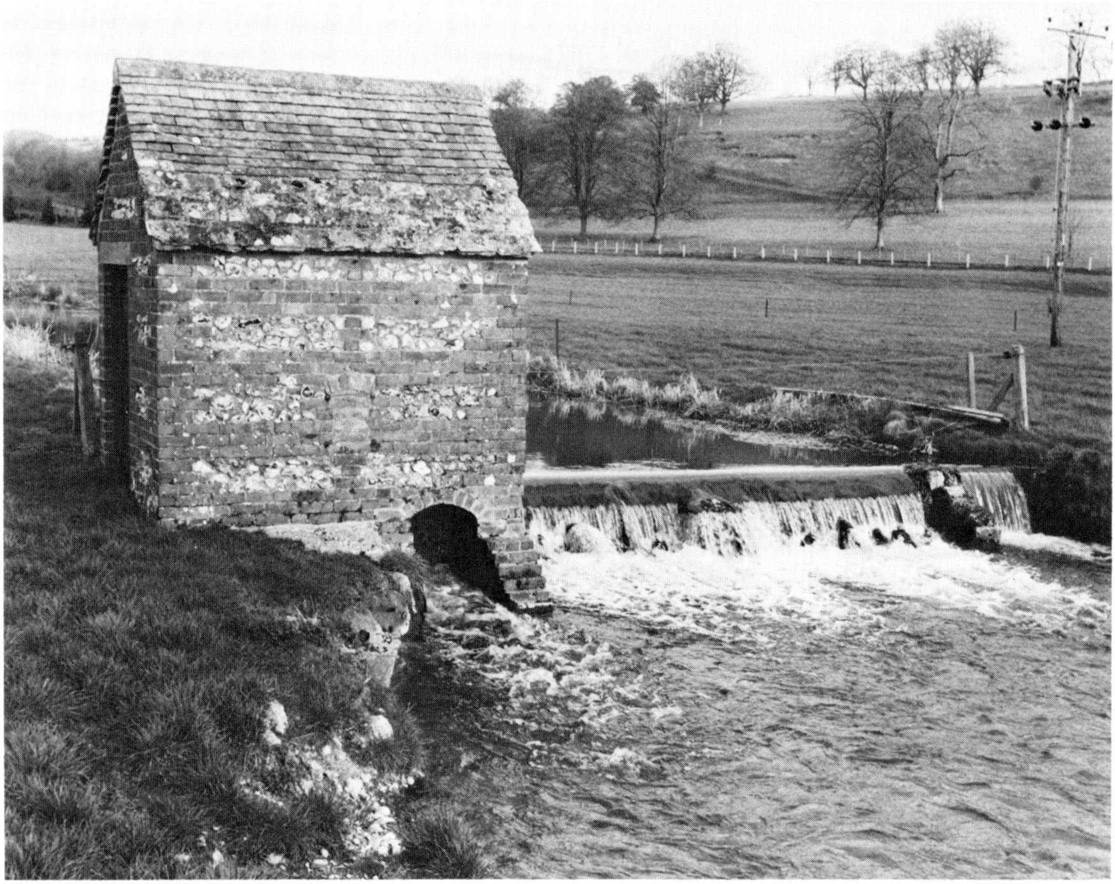

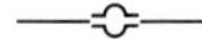

'. . . methinkes he is much more happy . . . that at ease contemplates . . . the wanton windings of a river . . . than he that with fire and sword disturbs the world. . . .'

Or watches for distant glimpses of imaginary invaders.

No one cuts watercress commercially at Steeple Langford now, we were told by a woman who came from her rows of vegetables and flowers to stare with us sadly at the overgrown cress-beds, but in small streams it was still cut by people to eat, she said, and someone 'in the Deverills' was cutting it and also breeding trout. Which in these areas seems like coals to Newcastle. (Near Wantage, at Letcombe Bassett, Hardy's Cresscombe of *Jude the Obscure*, the original cress-beds, possibly used from Roman times, are spring-fed from springs which come straight out of the bank at two or three yard intervals into the Letcombe Brook. 'Bassett Cress!' was an old

London street cry. The water is the same temperature all the year round, says Mr Tubb, who has been growing cress there since 1942. 'In winter, if your hands are really cold, the water's quite warm.')

In chalk streams, trout grow large. There is plenty of food – both surface insects and underwater food. In the alkaline water flora and fauna thrive, and water weeds such as crowfoot are natural aerators. The trout are healthy and of good colour.

> *The Chalk Stream gives best evidence of its quality in being the natural home of the trout and grayling, fish that do not often flourish in, and are never indigenous to, slow-running streams of other than chalk origin. There are two Avons in Wiltshire which illustrate the contrast to perfection: the one which runs westward through the fat pastoral regions, the clays and greensands of north-west Wilts towards Bath and Bristol; the other, which rises in the Marlborough Downs, and cuts through the heart of Salisbury Plain, as translucent as a mountain stream . . . alive with lusty trout—*[16]

Trout, king of the chalk stream. 'Mainly private', as I was told laconically at Steeple Langford, of the river fishing. In the lakes or pools, anglers indulge in coarse fishing.

Fashions in fishing, as elsewhere, change. In the days before dry fly fishing, 'local proprietors up and down the river [the Itchen, where with the Test the art of dry fly fishing was born, being with the Kennet the three most prized trout rivers; today the Hampshire Avon is relatively intact and therefore a prime river, its fauna especially diverse] gave their neighbours a day or two's fishing, no doubt, when they asked for it, as men do today upon obscure rivers. And the old-time sportsman, with no sense of a priceless favour conferred, went to work and cast his two wet-flies across and down the swifter streams, and took . . . his modest share of trout, pure-blooded lineal descendants of those the monks of Winchester netted for their stew ponds. . . .'[17]

An Edwardian commentary. But those who have fished in the 'obscure rivers' of Dorset and other counties (as well as with dry fly or nymph in less obscure chalk streams), can only think of trout fishing as Izaak Walton's 'most honest, ingenuous, quiet, and harmless art of angling', 'a procurer of contentedness'.

Fishing, from the downland coasts, also; paramount as a livelihood in early times. Fishing villages growing into fishing towns, such as Folkestone, where Defoe saw a 'multitude of fishing-boats', and the smacks which carried mackerel to London in 'a cloud of canvas'.

Even more vital, defence. Dover, the 'lock and key of the whole realm' of England, where the cliffs stand 'Glimmering and vast',[18] its hills a stronghold since Neolithic times, its castle keep impregnable (except to

Cromwellian troopers) from the time Henry II built it. The inhabitants along the shores of southern England, with its continually changing coastline – as towns became submerged or marshes dry land – seeing the comings and goings of kings, armies, abbots, refugees and ambassadors. Fearing the incursion of yet greater armies; seeing the Black Death slip in, which changed the face of the countryside, and later, more happily, foreign visitors to enjoy their spas and country pleasures.

From Bosham, Harold sailed to Normandy. At the beginning of the Bayeux Tapestry he is seen riding towards Bosham and then stripped to the waist as he wades to the ships, his hawk on his fist and his companions carrying hounds. To Shoreham came King John, when the death of Richard I left him King of England, and from there sailed 26 ships and 329 men for Edward III's invasion of France (more than from Dover, London or Southampton). Later, sailed forth privateers, pilgrim ships, frigates against the French or the Spanish Armada. From Shoreham too, King Charles II left, in 1651, after a flight, full of setbacks, along the coast, and a last night spent at Brighton, at the George (later King's Head) in West Street, where the landlord recognised him, and ran to kiss his hand, saying, 'It shall not be said but I have kissed the best man's hand in England.' (The ship Charles sailed in was the *Surprise*, and her captain, Captain Nicholas Tettersell, is buried in the churchyard of St Nicholas Church, Brighton's old parish church. As is that great Brighton character Phoebe Hessell, who enlisted as a soldier to follow the man she loved to war, without telling him or anyone else her sex; she later married him and, living to a characterful old age of over 100, was given a pension and saluted by the Prince Regent as 'a jolly old fellow'.)

But Shoreham, so flourishing in the days when the chequerwork flint and stone Marlipins building was a toll-house for the medieval de Braose lords of the manor, had even by the reign of Elizabeth undergone changes – 'by little and little fell to bee but a village . . . and gave encrease to another towne of the same name, where of the greater part also being drowned and made even with the sea is no more to be seene: and the commodiousnesse of the haven by reason of bankes and bars of sand cast up at the river's mouth quite gone: whereas in foregoing times it was wont to carrie ships with full saile as farre as to Brember.'[19] While Brighthelmstone, a much lesser place, having in the early sixteenth century a 'felde in the middle of the town' with 'hempshares' where hemp was grown for fishing nets, intersected by paths known – and still known – as lanes, was grown by Elizabeth's reign from a settlement of poor fishermen to one where four hundred men managed eighty smacks and ten thousand nets. But was not, for another century or two, rich.

> The place is really pleasant . . . such a tract of sea, such regions of
> corn, and such an extent of fine carpet, that gives your eye command
> of it all. . . . My morning business is bathing in the sea, and then

buying fish: and my evening occupation is riding out for air, viewing
the old Saxon camps [*sic*] and counting the ships in the road and the
boats that are trawling. . . .[20]
(1736).

Pleasant, but still poor, as another writer noted a few years later of the
'village on the sea coast' with inhabitants 'mostly very needy and wretched
in their mode of living'.[21]

Then the 1750's – Dr Richard Russell of Lewes advocates sea-water and
sea-bathing, and also discovers a chalybeate spring at Hove, which attracts
visitors.

1779. Fanny Burney writes in her diary, at Brighthelmstone: 'Mrs Thrale
says she lived upon the Steyn, for the pleasure of viewing, all day long,
who walked with who, how often the same persons were seen together,
and what visits were made by gentlemen to ladies, or ladies to gentlemen';
'. . . we found Lord Mordaunt, son to the Earl of Peterborough, – a pretty,

*Coombes Church,
Sussex*

languid, tonnish young man'; 'Mrs Cumberland, one of her sons, and both her daughters. . . . They are reckoned the flashers of the place.'[22]

Balls, parties, and conversation with the – to her – dreaded Dr Johnson, who was reported by Mrs Piozzi as declaring the neighbouring downs so dreary that a man would soon be so overcome by their dismalness that he would hang himself, if he could find a tree strong enough to bear the rope, but that he would not be able to find it.

The greatest Brighton flasher of them all did not despise the downs, however. First visiting his uncle, the Duke of Cumberland, there in 1783, at Grove House, the Prince of Wales was received by the inhabitants with a magnificent 'general illumination', every pane of glass in the town displaying a candle stuck in a lump of clay. The next day he and his uncle rode out with the staghounds. The following year he occupied the adjoining house of Mr Thomas Kemp, and later bought it, enlarging it to become his Marine Pavilion, with the Royal Stables begun in 1805.

For half a century Brighton was to be the most fashionable resort in Europe, and as Osbert Sitwell and Margaret Barton point out, 'The Downs, rather than the sea, appeared at this epoch to be the reason for the town's existence. . . .'[23] (those who wanted to bathe choosing in preference Ramsgate or Margate). During the final decades of the eighteenth century, all those interested in racing, hunting and coaching converged on Brighton. In 1805 the Prince bought the Prince's Dairy, a 'suburban' retreat on the London Road, where he kennelled a pack of harriers. Hunting received considerable impetus. The Duke of Richmond had also hunted his foxhounds in the neighbourhood of Brighton; villages such as Southwick were described in the eighteenth century as being 'prettily situated for hunting and shooting'. In 1783 racing had started on the downs at White Hawk (principally among officers of the Militia Regiments, under patronage of the Prince of Wales); another favourite pastime was cricket, on the Royal Ground, presented by the Prince to Brighton in 1791.

In 1784, the Duc de Chartres entered a horse for the Lewes races. One of the French patricians who began to flock to Brighton, he prided himself on introducing English fashions into France. Horace Walpole described his dress – 'he came dirty in a frock with metal buttons, enamelled in black with hounds and horses, a fashion I remember here above forty years ago'. But on returning to France, he invariably appeared in public, whether riding or not, in leather breeches, top boots and a pink coat. Young Frenchmen discarded their powdered wigs, took to wearing heavy English 'redingotes', and imported English racehorses, until Paris resembled 'a vast stableyard'.[24]

Following the fashionable visitors, came refugees from the horrors of the Revolution. One of the first was Madame d'Osmond, who had already met Mrs Fitzherbert in France, and whose daughter, the Comtesse de Boigne, in her memoirs refers to the pavilion as a 'masterpiece of bad taste'.[25] She is eloquent on the beauties of the English countryside: 'I do not think any other country can give an idea of the English countryside. One sees a different sky there, and breathes a different air. The trees have a different aspect, the plants different hues. . . . And there is no language in which the charms of the countryside are praised, in prose and verse, with a more lively and sincere passion than in English literature.' Anyone, she concluded, who had spent three months in London, would understand the 'physical relief one experiences on leaving it'. She tells of the Prince in Brighton riding every day from 3 o'clock, and of his kindness and considerateness to guests, always first in the room to greet them, showing them round – to admire his new kitchens in particular – seeing that they had everything in their rooms that they might need. When the Grand Duke Nicholas visited Brighton in 1817, the Regent arranged for him to be taken on excursions each day, to visit places of interest within a fifteen-mile radius. (A painting at Petworth House, shows the Prince Regent with the Grand Duke's brother, Tsar Alexander I, being received in the Marble Hall there by Lord Egremont, on the occasion of the Tsar's stay in England three years earlier.)

By this time, the Prince was separated from his wife the Princess Caroline. (Before she left England for Italy, she stayed for a while at Sompting, embarking at Lancing.) He had also parted once more from Mrs Fitzherbert, the strength of his devotion to this woman whom he had secretly married when he was 23, but more than once deserted, perhaps made most clear on his death, to Wellington who, bending over the dead King, saw a miniature of Mrs Fitzherbert on his breast. The King had not seen her for a long time, but neither he nor she, on returning other possessions, had given up the miniature of the other.

'Hail, thou purveyor of shrimps and honest prescriber of South Down mutton! There is no mutton so good as Brighton mutton; no flys so pleasant as Brighton flys; nor any cliff so pleasant to ride on; no shops so beautiful to look at as the Brighton gimcrack shops, and the fruit shops, and the market.' Thackeray, in *The Newcomes*. He stayed at the Old Ship, or Mutton's. To him, Brighton was 'London *plus* prawns for breakfast and sea air.'[26] 'The Chain Pier, as everybody knows, runs intrepidly into the sea. . . . You can watch the sun setting in splendour over Worthing, or illuminating with its rising glories the ups and downs of Rottingdean. . . .'[27] (The Ship Inn, Dover, was also fashionable in the eighteenth and nineteenth centuries. Chateaubriand was given a reception, as ambassador, there in 1822, and it was patronised by American and other visitors.)

The Brighton Chain Pier, completed in 1823, was of the new era. New, light mailcoaches, drawn by better-bred horses over macadamised roads, and in 1841, the opening of the London/Brighton railway line led to another peak of popularity for 'England's Favourite Watering Place'.[28] In 1806, the young Lord Byron had spent weekends (or 'Saturday to Mondays') at Brighton, boxing with 'Gentleman' Jackson, riding on the downs, or boating, accompanied by a girl dressed as a boy whom he called his 'brother' – a mistress housed opposite the Pavilion. By 1824, Hazlitt was writing, as he entered the town to catch a steam packet, 'The genius of the south had come out to meet us. . .', and in 1832, Cobbett stated in a letter: 'Brighton, certainly surpassing in beauty all other towns in the world; it is closely bounded on one side by the sea; surrounded on other sides by lofty and verdant hills, between which run valleys in every direction, covered with corn and flocks and decorated with lofty and beautiful trees. . . .' In 1848, Prince Metternich was commenting on the almost southern quality of the flowers and shrubs.

Lewes Crescent, Kemp Town, Brighton

In 1848–9, Brougham, Palmerston, Aberdeen, Macaulay, Bulwer-Lytton and Dickens were among distinguished visitors (the Bedford was Dickens's favourite hotel; among other places at which he stayed was Folkestone, where he exercised by climbing 'a precipitous cliff'); Mario and Jenny Lind sang, and Johann Strauss the elder conducted at the Town Hall. The Duke of Devonshire, who owned Compton Place and other properties at Eastbourne, gave balls; it was his successor, the seventh Duke, who finally developed Eastbourne as a model resort. Other resorts such as Worthing asserted themselves, as towns with their own commissioners; while, farther west, Melcombe Regis – now one town with Weymouth – which had, as had Weymouth, been a great medieval port taking advantage of Radipole Lake and the anchorage in Weymouth Bay, and had then declined in importance, grew newly fashionable, with the Duke of Gloucester visiting in 1780, and George III from 1789 until 1811, with still later developments of fine terraces until the mid-nineteenth century. The downs overlooking Weymouth Bay, so impressive a sight still with ships lying at Portland, are those described in Thomas Hardy's *The Trumpet-Major* – White Horse Down with its figure of George III on horseback, and downland villages: Bincombe, Poxwell (incorporated into his 'Overcombe'), and Sutton Poyntz.

> It was a clear day with little wind stirring, and the view from the downs, one of the most extensive in the country, was unclouded. The eye of any observer who cared for such things swept over the wave-washed town, and the bay beyond, and the Isle, with its pebble bank, lying on the sea to the left of these, like a great crouching animal tethered to the mainland . . . the sea . . . glaring like a mirror under the sun.[29]

Idyllically cottaged villages, or small hamlets in the dips of the downs; sunlight flickering through the trees on to a narrow lane or winding brook; doves and young sparrows flying up from thatch; porches drowned in foxgloves, sweet william, honeysuckle, periwinkle, pink roses and love-in-a-mist – places with names such as West Chaldon, Upton, Watercombe, Whitcombe, Broadmayne – and Osmington. Constable stayed at Osmington on his honeymoon, and painted the village several times, and Weymouth Bay – the 'wonderfully wild and sublime country around Osmington' which he always remembered, writing in a letter in 1823 from Fonthill, 'a wild region of the downs to the north, and distant Dorsetshire hills made me long much to be at dear old Osmington. . . .'[30] (It is interesting that he thought Sherborne church 'finer than Salisbury Cathedral', but considered 'Salisbury Cathedral from the Meadows' his best work.) For someone to whom 'Painting is but another word for feeling',[31] the downs, and the sea, held an appeal that towns could not offer. He stayed at Brighton for his wife's health, and painted there in 1824 'The

Gleaners, Brighton', showing two windmills on the corn-covered hills. He also painted the Chain Pier, and 'Brighton Beach with Colliers', inscribed on the back 'My dear Maria's Birthday. . . . Very lovely Evening – looking Eastward – cliffs & light off a dark grey effect – background – very white and golden light.'

He disliked the 'din and tumult' of the town: 'The magnificence of the sea, and its . . . everlasting voice, is drowned by the din. . . .'[32] At 58, he saw the country around Arundel for the first time, and was overwhelmed: 'The Castle is the chief ornament of this place – but all here sinks to insignificance with the woods, and hills. The woods hang from excessive steeps, and precipices, and the trees are beyond everything beautiful: I never saw such beauty in *natural landscape* before. . . .'[33]

Feelings echoed perhaps later by another creative spirit, Ivy Compton-Burnett, who referred to Hove as a 'horrid, horrid place', but from her youth there always remembered the swathes of wild flowers growing between the downs and the sea.[34]

'There is not a healthy man in London,' Constable had written. Many regions could offer escape, but the positive qualities of sea, air, landscape, and particularly light, have always attracted artists to a place such as Brighton. Richard Jefferies commented on the 'Bitter sea and glowing light', of a 'Spanish town in England';[35] Turner, Landseer, Sickert and Jacques Émile Blanche painted there – the last-named artist's painting of Black Rock, now in the tea gallery of the Brighton Museum and Art Gallery, epitomising, below white cliffs, the seafront of straw boaters and nursery nurses and children in long-legged striped bathing drawers. To Jefferies falls the summing-up of this curious town; his words apposite today: '. . . picturesque, red tiles, red chimneys, green jalousies, blue sky beyond, shadowy corners and archways. Bricks – pavements are very good until worn into holes. The pitchblack houses are disappearing gradually. . . .' 'The resolute way in which the Brighton people go about to spend their money shopping is worthy of admiration. . . .' 'There are rowing clubs and sailing clubs which neither row nor sail but are great at Poker. Of all the fashionable throng no one looks at the lovely sea. It is rather bad form in the drawing room society to mention it at all.'[36]

The sea – and horizon. The juxtaposition of downs and sea, or downs and water where small or wide rivers cut through the valleys; where breaker-like hills of grass meet cliff and waves, or dry scarps fringe a valley. An elemental landscape; not landscape at its wildest but at its most resonant. Space on space; an unfolding of the limitless. Between hills the sea; seen from a town, the distant hills on one side, crowned with a sea-horse of beeches, the Channel stretching to the other horizon. The changing light, which brings the downs to life; sun and cloud shadows moving over their

sullen whaleback shapes, licking their flanks with green fire, darkening gulleys, outlining the hills, at evening, with a brilliant metallic edge.

Qualities that have inspired writers as dissimilar as Tennyson and Virginia Woolf, Kipling and D. H. Lawrence.

Lawrence in 1910, to Louie Burrows: '. . . we walked over the cliffs and downs to Rottingdean . . . gulls flashing and daws gleaming, a great wide wake of sunlight slightly dimmed, oxidised with mist: a little wind. Rottingdean is a delicious village in the fold of the downs, gold with lichens.' Or from Hove: 'It has been a very sunny morning, with a mist like grey silk veils, and the sun-walk on the sea narrowing and darkening to orange and burnished copper and vanishing ruddily on the horizon into a closed door of fog.'[37]

Virginia Woolf, in 1927 and 1928, at Rodmell: 'the village standing out to sea in the June night, houses seeming ships; the marsh a fiery foam. . . .' 'We went to Amberley yesterday . . . an astonishing forgotten lovely place, between water meadows and downs'; 'something abstract; but residing in the downs or sky . . . Reality I call it.'[38]

A reality drawing visitors to the downland spas, and to present-day, sometimes over-developed riverside villages. Which has led us irretrievably to alter areas such as that built over by Peacehaven in Sussex, and some caravanned, charabanc'd resorts of the south, in our eagerness for enjoyment. So that what is now left, and daily threatened, needs jealously guarding. Not easy, since there are so many of us, and so little of our landscape left.

As early as 1926, Kipling wrote:

> *They take Our land to delight in,*
> *But their delight destroys.*
> *They flay the turf from the sheep-walk.*
> *They load the Denes with noise.*
>
> . . .
>
> *They string a clamourous Magic*
> *To fence their souls from thought,*
> *Till Our deep-breathed Oaks are silent,*
> *And Our muttering Downs tell nought.*[39]

They? we? our? None of it ours; but the heritage of all of us; a legacy to hand on. What is left is only a fraction of the scene that you see in an old painting or print of the downs, with the small hamlets on the edge of serene, bare hills crossed only by sheep tracks, peopled only by a shepherd, civilised only by a church or windmill. What will we, who are lucky to see this little left, hand on?

Village well, Long Crichel, Dorset

3

the happy ground . . . a dwelling for immortals. . .

William Blake

HOUSES AND MANORS AND HOW PEOPLE LIVED

Life, as anywhere else, was not always idyllic on the downs.

Richard Jefferies, who first attracted the public eye by an impartial letter to *The Times* in 1872, on the conditions of the Wiltshire agricultural labourer, saw this as clearly as anyone. Writing of 'the old days', in 'The Countryside: Sussex' – 'The granaries were full, the people half-starved. The wheat was threshed by the flail in full view of the wretched. . . . At night men tried to steal the corn, and had to be prevented by steel traps, like rats.'

Or describing the harvest:

> A human animal simply in all this . . . why should he note the colour of the butterfly, the bright light of the sun, the hue of the wheat? This loveliness gave him no cheese for breakfast. . . . His face grew red, his neck black; the drought of the dry ground rose up and entered his mouth and nostrils, a warm air seemed to rise from the earth and fill his chest. His body ached from the ferment of the vile beer. . . . The golden harvest is the first scene. . . . Bright poppies flower in its depths. . . . Behind these beautiful aspects comes the reality of human labour – hours upon hours of heat and strain; there comes the reality of a rude life, and in the end little enough of gain. The wheat is beautiful, but human life is labour.[1]

And in *The Story of My Heart* he cries, 'I hope succeeding generations will be able to be idle. I hope that nine-tenths of their time will be leisure time; that they may enjoy their days, and the earth. . . .'

Godmersham Park, below the North Downs, Kent

53

Or W. H. Hudson, in *A Shepherd's Life*:

That was her first place, and from that time on she was a toiler,
indoors and out, but mainly in the fields, till she was past 85. ...
Every morning thereafter Joan and her little brother, aged 7, had to be
up in time to get to the farm at five o'clock in the morning, and if it
was raining or snowing or bitterly cold, so much the worse for them,
but they had to be there, for Devil Turner's bad temper was harder to
bear than the bad weather.

A picture similar to that which Thomas Hardy, realist as well as
visionary, often describing a generation before his own, paints of Tess's
hard times on the downs, on an upland farm.

Here the air was dry and cold, and the long cartroads were blown
white and dusty within a few hours after rain. There were few trees,
or none, those that would have grown in the hedges being merciless-
ly plashed down with the quickset by the tenant-farmers. ... The
stubborn soil around her showed plainly enough that the kind of
labour in demand here was of the roughest kind. ... For hours
nothing relieved the joyless monotony of things.

Things which were no doubt much better than when Cobbett fulminated
against the break-up of the traditional rural economy. Agricultural enclosure, and the growth of new industries in towns, had already changed the
countryside. Then, after the Napoleonic wars, he deplored that those who
had profited from war continued to amass wealth:

It is manifest enough that the population of this valley [the valley of
the Avon] was, at one time, many times over what it is now; for, in
the first place, what were the twenty-nine churches built *for*? ... it
follows, of course, that the *fewer* poor devils you can screw, the
products out of, the *richer* the nation is. ...[2]

Enclosures, bad landlords, harsh game laws (seven years' transportation
for rabbiting on open land). In earlier centuries, bad communications, civil
war, disasters of climate and famine, the dissolution of monastic lands. In
the Middle Ages, plague, entering from the Weymouth area in 1348, and
endemic for about 300 years, leaving deserted villages. Harsh feudal laws,
succeeding the Norman invasion. Earlier still, the unrest of a disunited
England; Viking invasions; fire and destruction; an era in some respects
dark. The long years of prehistory, with changing cultures, ignorance of
crop rotation, a short span of perhaps brutal life.

At Whitehawk Neolithic Camp, parts of the brain pans of human skulls
were excavated in 1928, fragments of some having been charred in a fire.
All the individuals had been young at their death, the oldest not much over
20, and the youngest about 6. 'What', concluded the archaeologist E. Cecil

Curwen, 'were these children's skulls doing round this domestic hearth unless the occupant of this piece of ditch was a cannibal?'[3]

—◇—

In this lengthy time-span, the years of the Roman 'Peace' seem some of the most sunlit on the downs.

Bignor Roman villa – '. . . one of the most solemnly beautiful sites of South England, covering a general slope that looks right at the dark walls of the Downs.'[4] (Although the natives of Britain tended to till their traditional Celtic fields on the high downs, rich Romans, and the Romano-Celtic upper classes, chose sites at the foot of the downs, or in the coastal plains, for their villas.) In fine arable and cattle land still, mellow at harvest time, rolled bales of straw like draughtsmen in the fields; the line of Bignor Hill rising to the south, and to the west, Burton Down and Farm Hill, running into Barlavington Down. The villa site sheltered on its warm slope. Ash trees, summer flowers. Red-and-brown mosaics, corridors, piscina, areas for hot and cold baths, hypocaust, only a fraction of the one-time house which, with farm buildings, covered four and a half acres, round an inner courtyard – at the centre of an estate of two thousand acres crossed by Stane Street, the Chichester-London road. Windows would have been glazed with green glass, walls were decorated with painted plaster; chalk was used in the mosaics, and with flint in the exterior walls. Corn was ground with stone querns. There was probably a lambing pen, and accommodation for twelve plough-teams of oxen. Oyster, mussel and edible snail shells have been found there: Romans would also have eaten quantities of the vegetables which they introduced into Britain – radishes, beetroots, lettuces, cucumbers, chicory.

Roman villas were isolated farmhouses, standing among large, open fields. The native villages, or settlements, were surrounded by much smaller, enclosed fields, which are commonly called 'lynchets' (see page 108, Section 5). In areas such as the South Downs between the Adur and the Ouse, on Salisbury Plain, and in Cranborne Chase, settlements rather than villas predominated. On sites which may have been already farmed long before. But Roman farming gave a stimulus to the poorer settlements on the downs also. On Thundersbarrow Hill, on the South Downs, a village site was occupied from the end of the Iron Age until the end of the Roman period, with a large area of lynchets round the wattle huts, themselves near an old fort. Remains of two kilns or furnaces for drying corn were found there, with a flue beneath the roofed pits. (Both Pliny and Ovid mention this way of roasting or parching corn. Other Romanised manners in Britain are illustrated by finds of bone hair-pins, bronze ear-picks, part of a glass vase with traces of rouge. The poet Claudian cited two of the outstanding features of the country as Highland monsters and the use of rouge on the cheeks.)

Romans, and Romanised citizens, not only chose the sunny sides of hills for their homes, but also constructed their villas to catch the utmost sun, with a series of rooms running off a corridor, often in an E-shape without the central arm. Other incomparable sites near downland are for instance just north of Walton-on-the-Hill in Surrey, taking advantage of a south-facing slope not far from Stane Street, and not far also from the road from Headley to Juniper Hill, which, only minutes from the Box Hill pull-in on the A24, runs through some of the most pastoral country you – still – could find: green hillsides, lambs, beeches; hanger-like slopes on one side, hillocky fields on the other; fine park-like trees; all the fresh greens of spring with celandine and blackthorn; rabbits barely stirring as a car passes. Or at Danny, in Sussex, where there was a Roman villa, near the soft pyramid of Wolstonbury; a hill which now shelters Little Danny Farm with its old stepped pigeon-house walls. Or at Upper Upham near Aldbourne in Wiltshire, where a Romano-British site was covered by a village (later deserted), so that now only one fine seventeenth-century farmhouse bears witness to the continuing agricultural prosperity of some

Danny

two thousand years. Or at many other Wessex sites such as that north of
Badbury Rings, near Witchhampton.

———◇———

The picture which we reconstruct of the past is always changing. Ages
which were considered 'dark' are viewed as more civilised when new
aspects of culture or art are discovered. One century reads in depth of the
Roman world, the next of the Vikings. Preconceived ideas of geographical
and historical layout alter.

In 1981 a dramatic find, the finest and largest of its type this century,
came to light below the downs, near Bramber Castle in Sussex. A
spearhead hoard – eighty spearheads, with spear butt fittings, chisels,
knives, one socketed axe, bronze rings, and ornamental trappings,
emerged when a mechanical digger was at work in what was once the
flood plain of the River Adur. The first hoard of this type (Broadward –
dating to about 900–700 BC) to be found in Sussex, of a selection of tools
which may have been deposited in a watery area as part of some symbolic
ritual, it throws new light on Bronze Age culture. One of the nearest
comparable hoards was found near Winchester in Wessex, the region of
the great Bronze Age metropolises. At Bramber it was unexpected. Further
investigation could reveal much about life at that date, and about possible
changing water-levels.

So much of what we know of early history is founded on what we have
excavated; so much still lies buried. But the ever-splintering kaleidoscope
continues to change; the images shift, moving momentarily into sharp
focus.

The homes in which people lived, highlighting their world for us,
overlain by more recent history: houses over manors, homesteads over
forts, where primitive man ran with the wind in his ears.

The Old Stone Age – the first inhabitants coming over from the
Continent, hunters using rough flint weapons, still before the great Ice
Ages. As the glaciers retreated, bands of hunters and food gatherers in the
Middle Stone Age making clearings in the forests with fire, trapping beaver
and killing wild ox. In Dorset and along the Kennet Valley they fished and
hunted deer, in Sussex kept close to the hunting grounds of the clay
Weald. They were few in number – on Salisbury Plain perhaps only one
band of fifteen people.

Neolithic men, of the New Stone Age, bred animals, grew cereals, spun
and wove, made pottery. Drove their cattle into causewayed or entrance-
wayed camps, which were probably also for trading, ceremony or defence.

On the Trundle, near Goodwood, faint traces of a Neolithic cattle
enclosure or causewayed camp can be seen inside the earthen ramparts of
the later Iron Age hill-fort. (When it was excavated in 1928, among other
things were found bones of long-horned oxen, horned sheep, pigs, roe

deer and dogs; flints, oyster shells and a carved bone phallus.) Maumbury Rings on the outskirts of Dorchester is an example of a simple henge monument, or earthwork. (The circle was later adapted to make a Roman amphitheatre.) Other Late Neolithic enclosures, such as Durrington Walls, Mount Pleasant, Knowlton, were built for defensive reasons. Bands of aggressive herdsmen had moved into areas of open grassland in Wessex and elsewhere; competition for the best pastureland would have ensued.

The houses Neolithic men lived in were well-built timber homes like log cabins, about the size of a cottage. Neolithic man was intelligent, skilful in crafts and husbandry, but his life was short. Thirty-six was a good lifespan for many men, 30 for women. Most adults had arthritis; spina bifida was known and rickets common. Abscesses and inflamed gums led to loss of teeth. Four people in ten died before they were 20. Danger was on every side – from poisonous plants, wolves, wild boar, brown bears, men.[5]

The Beaker Folk, coming from the Low Countries, but originally from the eastern Mediterranean, having merged in northern Europe with people of another, 'Battleaxe' tradition from southern Russia, brought, in about 2400 BC, the first metal to Britain – copper-tanged daggers and knives, gold ornaments. They were traders, paving the way for the great traders of the Bronze Age. They may have kept bees, and made mead from honey – a potently intoxicating form of early mead, made from fragrant lime-honey, mixed with meadowsweet or other herbs. Traces of honey have been found in their beaker pots (flat-based and finely decorated). To make bronze, Cornish tin had to be brought along the trade routes of the Bronze Age, with Irish copper, and gold. Bronze Age people traded as far afield as the Mediterranean, and their culture merged with earlier ones. In Kent, Free Down Round Barrows (once an extensive group) lie along one of the trading routes between Wessex and the Low Countries – inside were found urns, incense cups, faience beads.

By the Iron Age, some of the best land was probably overcrowded. Hilltops were fortified. The technique of smelting iron was introduced. New invasions of Celts followed the earlier settlements of the Bronze Age, the last invaders before the Romans being the Belgae from north-east France and Belgium, who introduced coinage, wheel-turned pottery and the wheeled plough. Cissbury is perhaps the best example of an Iron Age fort on the South Downs; there are several others, such as that of the Caburn, or on Wolstonbury, and many in Wessex – Badbury Rings, Danebury and Maiden Castle, to cite only three, the latter an example of an earlier camp being fortified. At Butser Hill in Hampshire, at an ex-perimental prehistoric farm, plants and animals relevant to the time are studied and can be seen. In Kent, Bigbury Hill fort lies astride the Pilgrim's Way. In Surrey, there are many examples, although some are badly damaged.

The word 'down' comes from the Celtic *dún*, a fort or hill, often both.

With the Saxons, new images take over. The church, as Christianity spread, holding the scene until the dissolution of the monasteries. Already much of the high downs had been converted to sheep walk; upland villages became deserted, and Roman estates neglected. Minster churches, often with preaching crosses on their land, parish churches, monasteries, became the hubs around which life revolved. They were large landowners. (Now often only ruins remain, as at Shaftesbury where King Alfred founded a nunnery in AD 888 – perhaps the richest in the country. A country that was still war-torn: invasions continued until the ninth and tenth centuries. But the population of England probably doubled in size between the end of the Roman era and the Norman Conquest.)

Great royal estates, as well as monastic ones. The manor houses of lords took the place in the countryside which they would hold from then on. Saxon manors are elusive. (A few only are recorded: the burgh or borough of Arundel is mentioned as belonging to Alfred, as are other territories, particularly in Wessex.) With the Norman Conquest, and the Domesday Book, the picture becomes clearer. For instance, Roger de Montgomery, who had been created Earl of Arundel after the Battle of Hastings, was given eighty or so manors by William I, including land which had belonged to Harold.

Castles, to hold secure the lands of feudal lords. Remains stand or lie – below or above ground – as at Marlborough, Sherborne and Old Sarum, at Sherrington in the Wylye Valley, Bramber in Sussex, while Corfe stands as a gateway in the chalk, guarding the way to the Isle of Purbeck. Some overgrown motte-and-bailey castles are hard to find – at Edburton on the South Downs for instance – other castles are still magnificent, as at Lewes, where William de Warenne, the Conqueror's son-in-law and one of his most powerful lords, built his impressive fortress. (Features of his date survive. The name Lewes comes from the Old English *hlaew*, a hill.)

Meanwhile, on farmsteads, while sheep, cows and bullocks roamed the downs, barns were built to house men and cattle together, either on sheltered slopes or in valleys or coombs. An eleventh-century farmhouse consisted of living quarters on one side with, across a passage, a threshing floor (from which we get the word threshold), together with space for the stock. A granary would be in a loft above. An interesting theory has even been propounded that the dimensions of old cottages were by tradition based on a measurement of sixteen feet, the length necessary for a stall for four oxen. Materials used were local – flint, clunch (a hardened form of chalk; another material, cob, was a mixture of chalk and clay with straw), timber from woods or shipwrecks, thatch supported by curved crucks and tie beams. The living quarters gradually became separated from the barn proper, which would take its place with other buildings round a courtyard.

During the Middle Ages, magnificent tithe barns were built. Later, with the increase of small yeoman and tenant farmers, farm buildings became

smaller. Old barns had separate bays for each crop – hay, corn, root crops, wool after shearing. Village craftsmen through the centuries contributed to the building operation. There might be elaborate copings, pinnacles, gable-ends, windows. The blacksmith would make fittings and ironwork, hinges, locks, and the tools themselves – sheep shears, hay knives, sickles.

Stone barns, or barns of stone and flints mixed in alternating courses, knapped flints, or flints in a chalk marl, gave way in some areas to elaborate patterns of brick and stonework, or rubble and brick. The typical eighteenth- or nineteenth-century barn is a solid, imposing building, sometimes with dramatically sloping roof.

One of the longest barns in England, although half is now ruined, is the fourteenth-century tithe barn at Abbotsbury, 270 feet by 30 feet, with buttresses, mouldings and porched doorways, the air allowed to circulate through narrow slit windows. Used now to store locally grown reeds, with which Abbotsbury's thatched houses are roofed, the barn stands in an age-old setting by a pond thick with reeds and yellow flags, self-heal or carpenter's herb growing in the field that abuts it on the other side. The Benedictine monastery at Abbotsbury established the swannery in the Fleet. (Since the dissolution of the monasteries, the village has belonged to the Strangways family. In 1975 they received an award for their works of conservation. Craft industries have been re-established in the village.)

Such barns, and those of a later date, are still some of the most satisfying architecture in downland scenery, whether alone on the hills, or part of a farmyard group. In a green landscape, the ochre lichen on roofs, the solidity of flint or brick walls, provide a strong contrast, and even comparatively modern barns often blend well.

Of notable barns in downland, there are many in Dorset and elsewhere in Wessex, in the Tarrants and Winterbornes, at Thorncombe, Poxwell, Blandford, Cerne Abbas; in Hampshire at Buriton Manor House, in

Old farm buildings at Exceat in the Cuckmere Valley

Wiltshire at Stourhead, to name only two; in Sussex, at Exceat, Firle, and along the scarp; in Kent, Lenham tithe barn is an early example.

Other features of the landscape were water-mills, which were in use by the eighth century, and windmills, which with fulling mills appeared towards the end of the twelfth century – and have since been beloved by artists such as Constable, and often stand restored, on or near their original sites, as at Halnaker.

Dovecotes, also, were not merely decorative details of manor houses, but followed the pigeon-houses of the lord's demesne – square or circular, housing up to several hundred birds, to furnish fresh meat in the winter when other supplies were scarce. The birds wheeling with a flash of wings above an old farmhouse, or the doves roosting on the roof of a cottage, are of a longer tradition than plough horses or plashed hedges.

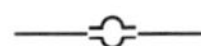

> ... you see here, as in Kent, Sussex, Surrey and Hampshire, and, indeed, in almost every part of England, that most interesting of all objects, that which is such an honour to England, and that which distinguishes it from all the rest of the world, namely, *those neatly kept and productive little gardens round the labourers' houses*, which are seldom unornamented with more or less of flowers.[6]

Village architecture reached a highpoint in the sixteenth and seventeenth centuries. Some skills (thatching, for example) still survive, especially in areas such as Dorset and Wiltshire.

Cottages of clunch and stone, chalk and thatch, of flint, brick-nogging, brick and timber. Flint-and-stone patterns as in the Wylye, Bourne and Avon valleys. Homely cottages and mills of the Kennet. Tiled clunch and brick walls at Aldbourne. Thatched walls at Over Wallop and West Kennet. Carved wooden gables at Mickleham in Surrey. A profusion of flint in Sussex, in houses, cottages, long flint walls. (In Kent, a mixture of materials, including half-timbering. No purely chalk villages because the Kentish chalk is porous and brittle, the downs capped nearly everywhere with clay-with-flints.)

Cottage gardens, too, the real cottage gardens, with the 'old, homely, cottage-garden blooms, so old that they have entered the soul',[7] relate most closely to those days. Medieval gardens concentrated on herbs, with a limited number of flowers which could be used for flavouring – violets, daisies, columbines (for soups). Even at the beginning of Henry VIII's reign, vegetables 'remained either unknown or supposed as food more meet for hogs and savage beasts than mankind'.[8] Then 'nosegaie gardens' were introduced, with flowers such as roses, lilies, clove-pinks and periwinkles, while in larger gardens, fruit trees were gradually banished to the walled kitchen garden. More exotic fruits and plants were imported during the sixteenth century, and Henry VIII's Italian craftsmen introduced the architectural or formal garden. So the true cottage garden, with its rows of vegetables and fruit trees interspersed with roses, pinks, sweet william, marigolds, even its little box hedges, seems to have been born before the fruit trees were banished, and to have taken for its own the miniature box hedges of the formal layout and some of the prettiest new flowers and most practical vegetables. Certainly it has nothing in common with the more elaborate gardens of the eighteenth century, or the dark shrubs of the Victorians.

With the Tudors, the feudal Middle Ages waned. Farms were enclosed and wool merchants flourished; both they and clothiers were able to build themselves comfortable 'middling' houses, of which Horace Walpole remarked the English had so many – 'I perceive now there is peculiar to us middling houses; how snug they are!' Many of these sixteenth-, seventeenth- and eighteenth-century medium-sized houses were near the chalk, particularly in the west, for example along the valleys of the rivers of Salisbury Plain. (Reddish Manor is a typical small-scale eighteenth-century manor house, at Broad Chalke. 'The best white cloaths in England are made at Salisbury,' it was held.)[9] The enclosure Acts and a boom in farming in the eighteenth century (then, and in the nineteenth century, food had to be provided for the growing cities) led to enlargement of the big farm houses.

By that time the graceful classical style had been introduced, particularly for great houses, but there is about most true downland architecture a feeling of being very close to its roots, and the countryside from which the owner's wealth derived. Landscaped parks had the near or distant hills as their chief ornament.

Although there was suffering from the loss of common fields and sweeping away of villages, big farms and estates did help to preserve the countryside in which any kind of country life could continue, and still in many instances, preserve it.

The continuity provided by estates can be strikingly seen at an estate such as Crichel in Dorset, where the inhabitants of the original village of More Crichel were rehoused to make room for the landscaped park and lake of the beautiful Palladian house of the 1760s (a seventeenth-century house having burnt down). Today the estate is still miraculously unspoilt, the latest buildings seeming to be the Mary Anna Cottages of 1950, at Long Crichel, in traditional style. All cottages have dark green paintwork; the farmland is well tended. Having been lucky enough to spend the war years at Long Crichel, in a farmhouse, I am amazed to find on going back that the landscape is unchanged. Pheasants still amble unconcerned across the roads; the stream runs clear between heads of nodding comfrey; the line of the old Roman road runs straight alongside wheat and plough, and by the side of the woods where beeches reach dark arms to the sun, some so tall they seem to form a mysterious circle. Here I saw traces of ash from truant bonfires, as if they had been there since we roamed this paradise.

Some estates have had more divided fates. The town of Shaftesbury was put up for sale by auction, early this century, and a high bid made prior to the sale by a property developer. Three prominent members of the county, however, bought the town from him, and so the walks of this hilltop town are preserved; also Gold Hill, with the best Georgian cobbles in the West Country. 'The city of a dream', as Hardy described it, although a dream more shattered in our day than in his.

Yet other estates have adapted in a more outgoing way to the trends of our times. At Goodwood on the South Downs, already famous for its race meetings, various commercial and leisure activities such as horse trials and international dressage have been developed, without spoiling the setting. Riding for the disabled also takes place there.

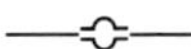

Newmarket Saturday

> I shall not be out of paine till I know how my dearest gott to London, and for that purpose I send this expresse to come away to morrow morning to bring me word how you have rested after your iourney. ... I should do my selfe wrong if I toulld you that I love you better than all the world besides, for that were making a comparison where tis impossible to expresse the true passion and kindnesse I have for my dearest dearest fubs   CR

Charles II, writing to his mistress Louise de Kéroualle, who had been lady-in-waiting to his sister the Duchess of Orleans.[10] She was sent to England after the Duchess's death, by Louis XIV of France, to keep Charles loyal to France. He was loyal to her, in that although he fathered thirteen or fourteen recorded illegitimate children (the first when he was nineteen) by various mistresses, when Louise bore him a son, he conferred on him in 1675 the titles of Duke of Richmond, Earl of March and Baron Settrington (also three Scottish titles); and Louise herself had become Baroness Petersfield, Countess of Fareham and Duchess of Portsmouth. The first Duke of Richmond's first shirt – nine inches high in old damask linen – is an intimately touching exhibit at Goodwood House, as is the baby-clothes' basket of King Charles I.

Goodwood is one of the supreme houses of the downs, outstanding perhaps not so much for James Wyatt's three wings of an unfinished octagon (part of the earlier house with its ionic columned Long Hall perfectly shows off Stubbs's famous paintings), as for the unmatched downland scenery of the park and estate, the fine stables with Tuscan arch and quadrangle (with squared flintwork cut by Napoleonic prisoners marched there from Portsmouth each day), and the trees, which from the time when the third Duke planted one thousand cedars of Lebanon have been carefully established, and include cork trees and sweet chestnuts.

Of fine houses in downland there are examples of every architectural era. Some, such as Firle Place near Firle Beacon, which stands with its pediment and attic windows almost like a French eighteenth-century château under the downs, face north, since in the old days (and there has been a house at Firle since the fifteenth century) it was thought that the south wind brought sickness and that the north and east winds swept it away. 'The south, as unkind, draweth sickness too near; The north, as a friend, maketh all again clear.'[11]

The village at Firle is quietly unspoilt. On Firle Beacon, as at the other beacon sites of the downs, fires have been lit at crucial moments of English history, in warning or celebration. In 1981 the beacon fire here was illuminated with fireworks, on the wedding eve of the Prince and Princess of Wales.

Village lane, Firle, Sussex

Again on the South Downs, Danny, under Wolstonbury Hill; the most romantic of houses, which Richard Jefferies called 'that curious old mansion, with its windows reaching from floor to roof'.[12] The mullioned glass of the Elizabethan house, in windows which span two storeys, catches the sun, and glistens in strange contrast to the massive simplicity of the downs, the unwalled fields which run as if to the front door.

The name Danny perhaps means 'the swine pasture in the valley'. 'Parham' is the 'pear-homestead'. The only Elizabethan house of its kind in England facing south (defying the rule), Parham has a quality of mellowness and warmth that is exceptional. Bowls of potpourri scent the rooms, of which one is a great hall. Upstairs, a long gallery runs 160 feet along the length of the house, panelled and sunlit, with a ceiling redesigned and painted with branches, birds and monkeys, by Oliver Messel. In its early

66

days it would have been used for walking, recreation, or even military exercise – the Parham Troop of Yeomanry was occasionally drilled here during the Napoleonic scares.

Under its warm stone facings, the house, in Elizabethan E-shape with later additions, is partly built of chalk; the staircase also rises round a large square of chalk (which material is very durable). Around the house, the gardens and park: the gardens being at present re-established in the original seventeenth-century pattern, with a trellis walk of vines and roses framing viewpoints into the orchard; in a niche in a wall where the pears of the pear homestead ripen, a stone goddess bears stone fruit; the park stretches away to the curving downs, across a lake and cricket field. Under the trees or across the drives, the unusual dark fallow deer stream in a flowing herd.

There is a ghost at Parham, heard, but not seen. No one speaks of it now, the gatekeeper told me. The house is evocative of many eras; memorable, too, for paintings – by Romney, Lely, Van Dyck – and for embroideries, arguably the finest collection in any house in England.

The original collector of many of the art treasures was the Hon. Robert Curzon, later fourteenth Lord Zouche. His wife was the daughter of Byron's cousin Robert John Wilmot and of Anne Beatrix Horton. It was to Lady Anne Wilmot Horton that Byron wrote the lines:

'She walks in beauty, like the night. . . .'

Built in later reigns (of James II and William and Mary), Petworth and Uppark are of the end of the seventeenth century.

Petworth Park is immortalised in Turner's series of paintings executed there for the third Earl of Egremont, one of the few aristocratic patrons to support the living artists of his day. At his funeral Turner walked at the head of a group of artists, before the coffin. He often stayed at Petworth, and his small paintings on blue paper in watercolour and bodycolour of some of the rooms at the house (now in the British Museum), show a music party, an artist with his easel and lady admirers, the famous white and gold room. In the house now hang the finished works of his paintings of the area – the lake at sunset; two white bucks fighting in another luminous view; farther afield, Brighton from the sea, with the Chain Pier; Chichester from the canal, spiked with reflections.

The rooms, halls, marbles are stately; wreathed carvings by Grinling Gibbons are 'the most superb monument' to his skill, in Horace Walpole's opinion. The estate dates back to an early Percy, and beyond. But the golden age of Petworth was surely that of the cultured third Lord Egremont, famous for his hospitality and 'delighting to reign in the dispensation of happiness' (Burke).

His feasts given for tenants and workers were legendary. A painting (by W. F. Witherington) shows the twenty-seventh fête in the park, held on 9 June 1835. Fifty-four tables each 50 feet long were arranged in a vast semi-circle on the lawn. Four thousand people were given tickets, but many more came. Extracts from Greville's Memoirs describe how food was carried round on hurdles, and 'Plum puddings and loaves were piled like cannon-balls in carts', while the old peer, who had been unable to give his winter feast because of illness, 'could not endure that there should be anybody hungering outside his gates, and he went out himself and ordered the barriers to be taken down and admittance given to all. They think 6000 were fed. ... It was altogether one of the gayest and most beautiful spectacles I ever saw, and there was something affecting in the contemplation of that old man ... rejoicing in the diffusion of happiness.'

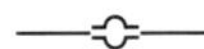

At Uppark, Emma Hart (later Emma Hamilton) was installed on the estate by her early protector Sir Harry Fetherstonhaugh, when she was sixteen. Here, later, H. G. Wells's mother was housekeeper, and Wells wrote that the place had a great effect on him.

The house is 'very neate', as Celia Fiennes remarked. A perfect, elegant, dolls'-house building, upright in red brick and white stone on its eminence of down, looking over varied downland scenery, and itself seen well from the height of Telegraph Hill to the south. Another lovely setting, at Godmersham in Kent, below wooded downs, where the Georgian mansion was built by the father of the man who made his cousin Edward Austen (later Knight) his heir, for whom Jane Austen, his sister, later sometimes kept house.

By the early eighteenth century, Vanbrugh was building houses such as Eastbury House at Tarrant Gunville in Dorset, completed for a famous eccentric, George (Bubb) Dodington, who invited there the poets, writers and politicians of his day (Fielding and Voltaire were guests). The ice-cellar for his lavish entertainments is overgrown by grass some way from the part which remains of the Vanbrugh mansion, which is perhaps all the lovelier for being as it were a fragment. Arcading laced with roses and jasmin shades the present front-door; the windows look out on the superlative vestiges of gardens once the glory of early eighteenth-century landscaping at the dawn of the style. Designed and laid out by Bridgeman, the gardens were perhaps the most important work he ever undertook, incorporating views over parkland separated from the more formal layout by his invention of the ha-ha. The walled kitchen gardens open one from another; in a greenhouse is, surely, the original ironwork and adjusting mechanism for roofridge and window catches; old-fashioned roses grow between the rows of fruit trees, their scent old as dark parchment. Outside, the vista of a rose walk; laurels and syringa; clumps of trees with their

Eastbury House,
Dorset

original layout still discernible in the long grasses of the park. From the top of the gateway arch grow two pine trees, which gives an idea of the scale of the original house, built to rival in size Castle Howard and Blenheim.

A later Georgian house, and smaller, but perfectly Palladian, is Came House, south-east of Dorchester. Carefully set on slightly rising ground, with portico and pediment bearing the Damer arms, and to one side a domed roof, it has the air of a house in a graceful stage setting.

Then the more elaborate landscapes such as that laid out by Sir Henry Hoare at Stourhead, with its lakeside circuit, and Capability Brown's masterpieces – to make room for which landowners didn't hesitate to cut new valleys, as at Charborough Park, or to remove villages like that of Milton Abbas. (We have Capability Brown's new model village of Milton Abbas in place of the old one.)

And imposing houses of later eras, such as the Victorian Bryanston House, near the town of Blandford, with its Georgian buildings put up after fire had devastated the town. Or towns where there is striking architecture of many periods, as at Lewes in Sussex, with its coursed,

69

knapped and squared flints, its brick-tiles, and grey bricks fired in the potash of coppice timber.

Houses, too, where there are the finest elements of may eras, as at Wilton, possibly the most sung, most renowned house of the chalk country.

An eighth-century priory, then an abbey in King Alfred's day, the lands at Wilton were given by Henry VIII to William Herbert, who had married the sister of Catherine Parr, Henry's last wife. 'The old building of the Earl of Pembroke's house at Wilton,' wrote Aubrey, 'was designed by an architect [Hans Holbein] in King Edward the Sixth's time. The new building which faced the garden was designed by Monsieur Solomon de Caus, tempore Caroli I, but this was burnt by accident and rebuilt 1648, Mr Webb then being surveyor.'

'The situation of Wilton House is incomparably noble,' he continued. 'It hath not only the most pleasant prospect of the gardens and Rowlindon Parke, but from thence over a lovely flatt to the city of Salisbury, where that lofty steeple cuts the horizon. . . .

'King Charles the first did love Wilton above all places, and came thither every summer. . . .'[13]

There too, had come Sir Philip Sidney, whose sister Mary was the third wife of the second earl. Sidney's *Arcadia* was written there – according to Aubrey many of the verses 'seem to have been writt by a woman', and he attributed them to Mary. Ben Jonson, Edmund Spenser and Christopher Marlowe also visited Wilton, and Shakespeare may have played in *As You Like It* there; may have written it at Wilton.

Philip, the fourth Earl, was a great lover of the arts, and patron of Van Dyck: '. . . he had the best collection of paintings of the best masters of any peer of his time in England.'

It is not known in fact if Holbein designed more than the entrance porch of the first house, but this still stands, some way from the house in the gardens – ethereal between trees. Nor would the other famous features of the grounds – Palladian Bridge, Triumphal Arch – be as striking as they are, without the soft background of Wilton's fountains, parterres and gardens, the not over-tamed course of the river Nadder, running on to join the Wylye.

—◇—

The Palladian Bridge, Wilton

While Henry VIII might hunt from his palace of Nonsuch, or Elizabeth I stay at Wilton, the well-to-do citizen did not associate travel with holidays until the eighteenth century. Pilgrimages were made; festivals and family occasions celebrated; but travel over uncomfortable roads in slow vehicles was not lightly undertaken. However, health, if not happiness, was regarded seriously, and by the seventeenth century the spa at Epsom had been discovered. An account by John Toland, in 1711, conjures up the daily life of the spa, and the verdant nature of Surrey at that time.[14] The downs have seldom been so attractively portrayed, with their grass 'finer than Persian carpets'.

> EPSOM . . . is deliciously situated . . . the finest *Downs* in the World on the one Side. . . . The Downs, being cover'd with Grass finer than *Persian* Carpets, and perfum'd with wild Thyme and Juniper. . . . And for Sheep-Walks, Riding, Hunting, Racing, Shooting . . . they are no where else to be paralell'd. . . . EPSOM never misses of the Eastern or the Western Sun. . . . Behind the Houses are handsom, tho' not large, Gardens, generally furnish'd with pretty Walks, and planted with Variety of Sallads and Fruit-Trees. . . .

> At night, the ladies tripped from one dancing spot to another:

> Here the British Beauties, like so many animated Stars, shine in their brightest Lustre. . . . Here every old Man wishes himself young again, and the Heart of every Youth is captivated at once. . . .
>
> You wou'd think your self in some enchanted Camp, to see the Choicest Fruits, Herbs, Roots, and Flowers; with all Sorts of tame and wild Fowl, with the rarest Fish and Venison, and with every kind of Butcher's Meat; among which *Bansted-Down* Mutton, is the most relishing Dainty. . . . The Ladies, who are too lazy, or too stately; but especially those that sit up late at Play, have their Provisions brought to their Bed-side. . . .

He also refers to Box Hill: 'the enchanted Prospect of *Box-hill*, that *Temple of Nature*, no where else to be equall'd for affording so surprizing and magnificent an Idea both of Heaven and Earth. . . .'

Aubrey, too, refers to Box Hill, which even in his day was getting a little part-worn. 'The great Quantity and Thickness of the *Box* Wood yielded a convenient Privacy for Lovers, who frequently meet here . . . the Wood is much decayed now. . . .'

In 1700, James Brome, Rector of Cheriton in Kent, was writing a book of travels. 'So that since England is not destitute of those many taking Things which all Travellers so passionately admire Abroad, it is very incongruous to pretend to be acquainted with other Countries, and to be Strangers to their own, which is the Epitome of all other. . . .'

He set out 'When the Spring had rendered the Roads passable, and the Country was a fitting Entertainment for Travellers', and describes: the stones at Stonehenge – 'they will (say some) heal any Wound. . .'; Surrey – 'Tis adorn'd in most places with very stately Palaces of Gentlemen and Merchants'; Guildford – 'full of fair Inns'; Berkshire – 'adorned with woody Hills, and thick Groves, and fruitful Valleys, whereof that which is called the *Vale of the White Horse* is extremely delightful'; Dorchester – 'formerly a noted Place for the Manufacture of Cloth, as it is still for Sheep'; Badbury – 'a little Hill upon a fair Down'; Sussex – 'the Downs by the Sea side standing upon a fat Chalk or Marle are abundantly fertile in Corn'; Bourn near Seaford –' a place very Famous for its Wheat-ears, which are a sort of Birds in Summer very palatable and delicious, and so Fat that they dissolve in the Mouth like Jelly.'

Travel was in general edifying, and sociable. But by the end of the century, from 1770 to about 1830, communion with nature came into its own, and solitude was a requirement. Nature had been admired as a source of virtue, of innocence, but now began to be seen as a source of strength, something which Mark Girouard has described as 'a positive force, something which one could plug into and get a spiritual charge from'.[15] Paintings of country houses no longer showed an elegant throng of people; a single figure, of horseman or ploughman, would ride or walk through the landscape in idyllic isolation. People studied nature in more detail, and walking itself became acceptable as a pastime; no longer considered eccentric, it received its ultimate accolade in 1856, when the Prince of Wales, then 14, was sent on a somewhat dour tour of Dorset with his tutor and an elderly colonel.

Other travellers have left their own accounts of the manners and sights of England (Johann Wilhelm von Archenholz, Heinrich Heine, Montesquieu). Carlo Gastone Rezzonico commented on the comfort of life in England (in 1788), as did Prince Pückler Muskau later. House-parties in country houses were becoming more usual – at first as political gatherings or for race-meetings, but later for both sexes as social gatherings and for match-making, with balls, card-parties and country pursuits. The house-party would continue in many guises, with in the Victorian era hostesses such as Lady Ashburton at New Alresford entertaining Tennyson and Carlyle, and in the Edwardian, when house-parties perhaps reached their apogee, hostesses such as Mrs Willy James, who entertained Edward VII at West Dean. (In our own day, opera at Glyndebourne provides an opportunity to appreciate music in an idyllic downland setting, in the wholehearted way in which earlier society took its elegant pleasures.)

The English, as Emerson pointed out, went 'to their estates for grandeur'. Nor had tenants and the less privileged country dwellers been entirely excluded from a better standard of life. As landowners became conscious of 'improving' their estates and farms, the lot of their tenants

was often bettered. And they were included in festivities, such as those at
Petworth. On the other hand, there were many double standards. The
harsh game laws of early centuries were followed by poor laws, imprison-
ment without trial, more or less autocratic government.

It was not until the latter half of the nineteenth century, with the coming
of the railways, that the ordinary citizen could begin to enjoy the
countryside to a much wider degree, with day excursions, or holiday trips.
And it was not a rural peasantry, but an urban movement, which halted
the enclosure of the last common land between 1865 and 1875, with the
Commons Preservation Society.

> *But many a dingle on the loved hillside,*
> *With thorns once studded, old, white-blossomed trees,*
> *Where thick the cowslip grew, and far descried*
> *High towered the spikes of purple orchises,*
> *Hath since our day put by*
> *The coronals of that forgotten time;*[16]

The downs in areas such as Surrey, which had for so long remained
unspoilt, with medieval hunting preserves, followed by the mansions of
rich magnates, were built over, much of their prehistory ploughed up,
their leafy beauty hacked down, although in corners remaining still.

So the picture has continued, with new roads, new suburbs, new infill,
encroaching on our hump-backed hills. Pylons stand aggressively on the
skyline (as above the Adur Valley). Oil has been found in Dorset – 'The
thin end of the wedge' a man who can see the Wytch Farm field from his
bedroom window, told me. (One rig eight years ago, now other drilling
sites, with applications to drill in further areas of hills and heathland.)
'Progress, that is,' he said sadly.

Surveyors quarter the Sussex downs with their ominous flags. As well as
the proposed Brighton bypass, the village and countryside of Steep in
Hampshire is with other villages threatened by one of several suggested
routes for a Petersfield bypass, both roads being strongly opposed by those
who love the downs.

'Forget the spreading of the hideous town; /Think rather of the packhorse on the down' wrote William Morris, in the Prologue to *The Earthly
Paradise*, in 1868.

It is no longer enough to be nostalgic.

'It's strange how the problems are always the same,' a member of the
Society of Sussex Downsmen told me. (They drilled for oil in the 1930s, too.)

A pioneer preservation society, it was formed in 1923 by a group of
downland walkers who saw a need for conservation; there was at that date
little or no town planning.

Burmester Hall,
Mickleham, Surrey

1926. 'Representations were made to the Brighton Town Council in connection with the proposal to establish a Film Studio Scheme in the Whitehawk and Sheepcote Valleys' (3rd Annual Report).

Another early battle was against a motor-racing track at Portslade, that was proposed no less than three times at different dates. The Downsmen successfully opposed it. At the same period, they were receiving many complaints 'from walkers, riders and landowners about the number of motors run on to the open grass'. This is again a matter much in their minds. Some Roads Used as Public Paths (RUPPs) are old tracks not suitable for cars; there is an increase of motorcycle traffic on rights of way.

An important achievement in the early days was when in 1926 it was realised that unless immediate action was taken, there was a strong probability that the Seven Sisters, one of the finest cliff walks in England,

Blossom on the North Downs

would be built over. The Crowlink Valley (Seven Sisters) was purchased for the nation by public subscription, led by the Society, and was then transferred to the National Trust, remaining one of our few unspoilt coastal areas.

War has been waged on overhead electricity cables, rubbish-dumping, tree-felling, the diversion of footpaths, ugly refreshment booths. Downland clearances are made, and the proper use of the downs promoted.

Support of such societies, which are active in practical as well as vocal ways, gives us perhaps our best chance of preserving the countryside.

Harvest, near Bignor, Sussex

— 4 —

the trail where the shepherds pass . . .

John Galsworthy

RIDGEWAYS TRACKS ROADS · RACING HUNTING AND SPORT

Older than shrines, habitations, battle sites. 'They are the serpents of eternity . . . the roads are the only things that are infinite,' wrote W. B. Yeats.[1] The age of the oldest roads is uncertain: they are linked, overlain by more modern ones. As Edward Thomas said, 'The earliest roads wandered like rivers through the land, having, like rivers, one necessity, to keep in motion.'[2] And many of those unchecked rivers take their course along the ridges of the chalk downs.

Cattle or sheep on the slopes of a downland pasture, winding their way round a hill, step into the track trodden down by the animal in front of them, by other animals weeks before. In wet weather their hooves sink in, a wall of chalk, flint and mud is built up at the edge of the track, making a terrace-way; in dry weather it hardens; the sides of the hill become scored by a succession of paths. Even rabbits scour their own trackways. Early men needed only instinct to follow the obvious routes; it perhaps does not matter if we shall never know whether a particular section of an old road was first used by wild ox or man; whether a green lane is of medieval or Roman date. Like streams too, these dry waters have converged and meandered, divided and changed course, been solidified or dammed, and in all the stratified history they represent, lie some of the profoundest and richest sources in an exploration of the past, and the inspiration for some of our finest literature.

To-day I know there is nothing beyond the farthest of far ridges except a signpost to unknown places. The end is in the means – in the sight of that beautiful long straight line of the Downs in which a curve is latent – in the houses we shall never enter, with their dark secret

The Ridgeway, Overton Hill

79

windows and quiet hearth smoke, or their ruins friendly only to elders and nettles – in the people passing whom we shall never know though we may love them. To-day I know that I walk because it is necessary to do so. . . .[3]

—◇—

'a sheaf of half a dozen footpaths worn side by side. . . .'[4] Many prehistoric trackways were almost certainly originally made by large-scale migrations of wild animals in the centuries following the end of the last Ice Age. Such a track, made by migrating cattle, may have been the origin for instance of what is now called the Pilgrim's Way. As large herds were involved, the tracks were broad and straggling, fanning out over the countryside, only narrowing at river fords or other obstacles, and being joined by countless lesser paths, as later on, lanes would join a larger road.

From four different angles, great ancient highways of the south converged on Salisbury Plain, running along the chalk uplands. The Ridgeway itself is older than Avebury, and the hill-forts which lie along it. Like the other routes, it was a means of communication and later of trade, and since many of prehistoric man's trading goods came from the east or west of the country – tin from Cornwall, jet from Yorkshire– the routes did not end at Salisbury Plain, but crossed it or joined one another there. Hilaire Belloc clearly set out the logic of following the chalk ridges in *The Old Road* (Pilgrim's Way).

> There runs from the neighbourhood of the Straits of Dover right across south England, in a great bow, a range of hills which for its length, unchanging pattern and aspect, has no exact parallel in Europe . . . a moderately steep, dry, chalky slope, always looking full towards the southern sun. . . . The end of each day's march is clearly apparent from the beginning of it, and the whole is seen to lie along this astonishingly homogeneous ridge. . . . You may say that from the Straits of Dover to Farnham, Nature herself laid down the platform of a perfectly defined ridge, from which a man going west could hardly deviate, even if there were no path to guide him.[5]

The present-day walker has the advantage of being guided along the ridgeway paths by the Countryside Commission's long-distance footpaths, expertly mapped, and waymarked by county councils. To walk along them is rewarding; but even those who are not long-distance walkers can experience the mysterious elemental pull of the old roads; can look along the chalky paths thickly edged with grasses and wild flowers, or along rain-washed rutted flint tracks as they disappear in shrouds of summer mist towards an unknown horizon. On the wildest stretches the ribbons of paths lie along the crests of the downs. The wind howls around them.

Elemental sensations; elemental regions.

*Wolstonbury Hill –
looking towards Jack
and Jill*

In Cranborne Chase, having climbed up by the old Smuggler's Lane, which is undoubtedly older than its name, and followed the modern road to Fontmell Down and on to Win Green, looking down into dizzying coombs, above the flight of kestrels. On the White Horse Downs, from the Ridgeway Path, looking down through the topmost branches of clinging beeches northwards to a blue distance, which on a clear day is said to stretch as far as Birmingham. After a thunderstorm, crossing the same path from the side of Hackpen Hill, with a rainbow setting over the Hackpen white horse; emerging on to a plateau which has all the calm majesty of the Marlborough Downs at their best; dark distances outlining the great dun and ochre sweeps of land, with lines of soot-black stubble after harvest, incandescent grasses caught in the sun, setting in the west beyond the outline of Windmill Hill. In the other direction Barbury Castle; clumps of trees to counterpoint the green curves and strange field-systems of a scarp.

81

A land of hope and glory. The path on either side.

> All day the wind, and often rain and wind together, roared in the trees. . . . The pale flowers were soaked and frayed and speckled with dust from the trees . . . under the wild, shadowy swoop of the mist and rain . . . we drank in the blue sky and the dark revealed tracts of plain and hill that lay stunned and astonished like a dreamer opening his eyelids after tumultuous dreams; we drank them with easy joy as of a man reading a great adventure when the heroes of it have long been dead, for we ourselves were so much above all that expanse which, powerless and quiet, might almost seem to belong to the past or to a tale.[6]

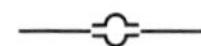

The ancient ways of the chalk.

The Harroway. The 'hoar' or ancient, or possibly the 'hard' way. From Dover along the North Downs to Farnham and on to Salisbury Plain. From Dover, the way originally went along the cliffs to Folkestone and then turned inland. Later, the Dover–Canterbury link became part of the way; the Canterbury–Winchester stretch became what is now known as the Pilgrim's Way. Pilgrims from England and Europe flocked to Canterbury to the shrine of Thomas Becket, their numbers reaching a height towards the end of the fourteenth century. The name Harrow Way is now usually reserved for the Farnham to Stonehenge stretch, some of which is difficult to trace.

The Great Ridgeway. A cross-country route from Brandon and the Wash to Axmouth in Devon. It crossed Salisbury Plain from the Wylye Valley to Imber, which is now closed by the army, and on via Win Green, Bulbarrow and High Stoy. The best known stretch is over the White Horse Downs, where it runs above the line of the Icknield Way: '. . . a battlement walk of superhuman majesty'.[7]

The Icknield Way is much mentioned in Anglo-Saxon Charters. It runs from East Anglia to the south-west, and may in many places have been a Romanised summer way of the Great Ridgeway. It is the name usually applied to the Great Ridgeway sections beyond the Thames (north-eastwards).

The South Downs Ridgeway. Logic points to the fact that the track or tracks along the South Downs from Beachy Head and on to Old Winchester Hill joined up with the other ancient ridgeways, of which there were many, including the Inkpen and North Hants Ridgeway, which ran via Inkpen and Walbury Hill (the highest chalk hill at 974 feet), to Basingstoke; the Dorset coastal ridgeway; the Wansdyke Ridgeway; and the Ox Drove Way from Win Green along the northern scarp of Cranborne Chase and on towards Winchester, although many stretches are composed of several trackways, and the name itself points to its later use by cattle drovers.

The Ridgeway Path. 137 km, from Ivinghoe Beacon by way of the Chilterns, the White Horse Downs and the Marlborough Downs to Overton Hill on the A4 west of Marlborough. Deviating at some points from the actual Ridgeway, for practical reasons or better walking. On or near the path can be seen, for example, Segsbury Camp, the White Horse and Uffington Castle, Liddington and Barbury Castles, Grey Wethers (sarsen stones) on Overton and Fyfield Downs, and Avebury.

The North Downs Way. 227 km, from Farnham to Dover, with alternative routes in the east, one taking in Canterbury. On or near the routes are Shakespeare Cliff, Jullieberrie's Grave, Kit's Coty House and the Coldrum Stones, the Roman villa site at Otford, Chevening, dene holes, chalk pits and hearthstone mines; Box Hill, Walton-on-the-Hill and the Hog's Back.

The South Downs Way. 129 km, from Beachy Head via the Seven Sisters or Jevington, along the South Downs to the West Sussex/Hampshire border near Buriton. On or near the route are Firle Beacon, Southease (or an alternative route via Glynde, Mount Caburn and Lewes), Ditchling Beacon, the Devil's Dyke, Chanctonbury Ring, flint-mine site at Cissbury Ring, Bignor Roman villa, Butser Hill.

The Wealdway. 42 km, from Gravesend to Eastbourne – crossing the North and South Downs, rather than being a ridgeway. It has taken ten years to complete and was opened in September 1981.

The Dorset Coastal Path from Lyme Regis to Poole Harbour, with an inland alternative route round Weymouth. (Interrupted by two firing ranges, so it is necessary to check firing times before walking, or to make a detour.) 116 km.

Roads upon roads, under other roads. Tracing them locally can be fascinating.

Most easily recognisable, since they were straight and, before Macadam, hard-surfaced, are the Roman roads. Across downland from centres such as Dover, Silchester, Old Sarum, Badbury, Dorchester. The fine stretches one motors along to the north-west of Winchester, or leaving Dorchester westwards. Roads the Romans laid out by aligning poles, or lighting braziers at night to be seen from point to point over hilly country, but bypassing such obstacles as the Chute Causeway in Wiltshire, or Silbury Hill, or re-aligning as Stane Street does to pass through the Mole Gap near Dorking. One of the best survivals in the country is the Ackling Dyke from Old Sarum to Badbury, adopted for a short stretch by the A354, its agger or embankment at places still at a height of many feet, its surface of varying materials. Where it crosses the Dorset Cursus on Wyke Down, imposing its powerful presence on the older landscape of barrows and prehistoric ways, but reclaimed by grasses and wild mignonette, a milestone of later, turnpike days pointing down it.

Saxon roads or tracks, their 'wegs' and military 'herepaths', are less easily traced. The well-known stretch of herepath connecting Avebury with the Ridgeway, probably continued on to Marlborough, for instance. Saxons used the Roman roads, and their own green lanes, or chalk tracks. The winding roads under scarps, such as the underhill lane on the northern scarp of the South Downs, east of the Adur, would certainly have been the link between Saxon settlements. It is echoed in another county by the under-scarp road below Wayland's Smithy on the White Horse Downs, where the scarp is curiously waved in an almost unearthly manner, catching light on its regular downrunning folds, which suck back like the tide from the plateau into which they drop.

The pattern of our roads, except for the most recent, was set by the eleventh century; they have only changed in importance. The character of early ones, of medieval lanes and holloways, can be judged from the rutted and terraced chalk tracks still used by farmers and walkers, or the hidden tracks, beloved of smugglers and easily climbed by a sure-footed horse, which run up a scarp under cover of beech branches. The tracks which shepherds used, the fanning droveways and the bald stretches of enclosure roads – made when open land was squared into fields – are a large part of the history, the character of downland, the spine and bones of a simple, unrarefied landscape, that might otherwise be too bland.

'We journeyed over Alpine mountains, drenched in clouds. . . . Sussex is a great damper of curiosity. . . .' So Horace Walpole. And before him Leland on Sussex roads full of 'dyrt and myre'. Or later, Cobbett's descriptions of slithering down Hampshire hangers or struggling along roads 'at once, road and river'.

Before the Tudor age, packhorses were the usual means of carrying goods (there are many fine packhorse bridges across rivers of the downs). Coaches mounted on springs appeared in the eighteenth century, but the first turnpike roads were opened in the reign of Charles II. (Charles's carriage once overturned twelve times between Whitehall and Petworth.) Turnpike Trusts took toll fees to be used for the upkeep of roads. (A small white-painted toll-house stands on Tarrant Hinton down on the A354, which follows the line of the Great Western turnpike road. Near here too, are pre-metric signposts to '6D Handley' – Sixpenny Handley – and at Tarrant Gunville one of the old AA signs, which, with old milestones, are so evocative of their respective eras.)

In true country districts inns are still, over long distances, the only providers of shelter and food; still overflow with bright brass tools and ornaments, old insignia, signed mementoes, prints of the squire in hunting dress, decorative pieces of china, antimacassars. Warm country voices still greet you, are still prepared to gossip or inform. Coaching towns, too, have kept vestiges of a particular elegance and purpose. Marlborough, on the old London–Bath route; its wide main street, fine inns, colonnaded shops, its 'Blowhorn Street' and Green. (Part of Marlborough College was once a coaching inn, the Castle, despatching forty coaches a day.) Dorchester, where the Antelope still styles itself a 'Coaching House' on its bills, promising to provide excellent horses and 'well aird beds', lock-up coach houses and 'select stables'. On the London–Brighton run, famous since the days when the Prince Regent covered fifty-six miles in four and a half hours in his phaeton, among notable inns were the Swan at Reigate and the White Hart at Godstone Green (later Clayton Arms). Passengers had to walk up hills in early coaching days (and push in heavy weather). They did, however, have plenty of refreshments, stopping for elderberry wine – 'roking hot' brought from a cottage on the Banstead Downs – or for gin and gingerbread, then lunch at Reigate, dinner of rabbit pudding farther on, 'neat liquors' at Handcross, tea at Patcham after walking up Clayton Hill.

The railways caused the run-down of the turnpike roads. Meanwhile, terrace ways and green lanes had been kept in use by drovers and others wishing to avoid paying tolls. The chalk surface was good for unshod animals, and they could graze as they went.

With the advent of cars, the emphasis changed once again. But it is interesting that historians of the evolution of roads have stressed both that their evolution was mostly by adaptation rather than direct planning, and also that as early as the sixteenth century a vicious circle began, by which when new roads are made they generate their own traffic: road improvement leading to increased speed and greater volume of traffic, which lead to demands for further roads, more improvements . . . more traffic. . . .[8]

'Leisure, fortune and the lure of sport – these things are implied in English society at every turn.'
(Henry James)

> *. . . their hounds, their horses, and their daring youth; . . .*
> *the wily fox, their furious chase shall be. . . .[9]*

Tracks, and race tracks. Chalk, being porous, drains easily and dries quickly. Sport has flourished on the downs.

It would be hard to say at what date hunting for pleasure began to run alongside hunting for food and skins, – surely from the earliest times. King Alfred is said to have had a deer park and to have kept a stud of horses at Ditchling. Saxon and Norman kings formally promoted the chase; William the Conqueror is known to have 'loved the deer like a father'. His successor, William II, introduced the death penalty for killing a deer illicitly.

From then onwards, deer parks became common, owned by king, nobles or clergy, deer being preserved for food, especially for fresh meat in winter, and for sport. By the nineteenth century, nearly every large landed

estate had a deer park, but their purpose was by then partly – or solely – ornamental. Charborough House in Dorset, with its magnificent stag gate, and park which was enlarged to 800 acres, is a good example of development. In 1838 there were 600 fallow deer there; about twenty years later a famous run took place, when a roe buck was pursued for four hours in pouring rain to Poole and back. Two pairs of wild boar were even introduced into the park – one from France and the other from Russia. They proved too savage and had to be killed off. The park still carries deer. In West Sussex, the deer of Petworth Park, one of the largest herds of park fallow deer in the country, are noted for their fine antlers. The castle of the Percys, which preceded Petworth House, had already been famous for the best stable 'of any subject in Christendom ... affording standing in state for threescore horses'.[10]

In Cranborne Chase, near Tarrant Gunville, is perhaps the best preserved of the many old medieval deer parks, Harbin's Park. An area of 115 acres enclosed by a bank and internal ditch, the bank now overgrown and overwooded but still discernible. Originally fencing would have topped the bank, just high enough to allow a deer to leap into the park, but because of the ditch, not out again. Here, if you are lucky, you may see a roe deer briefly outlined for an instant before it vanishes into the coppice to feed on the 'vert', the vegetation – such as holly and ivy, for their berries, and young hazel shoots – which in the days of forest and chase law was preserved as jealously as venison. At certain seasons of the year villagers would have been allowed to graze domestic animals and cut timber in parts of the Chase. In the undergrowth and hedges round Harbin's Park grow a mass of white campion, dog-roses, golden saxifrage and herb robert; also valerian or all-heal, for which Cranborne Chase was famous in the eighteenth century when its roots were much used in medicine by London druggists.

This area of the Chase is a mysterious, densely primeval region. There are thick dark woods in Stubhampton Bottom; deep gullies around Bareden Down; by Rolf's Wood roe deer; along the roads, red-legged partridge or a line of pheasant chicks pale as grass seed. Near Ashmore, some years ago, a sober-headed young man saw, in broad daylight, a procession of people in medieval dress, with rich trappings to their horses, with one man who was clearly a king. They passed onwards through the woods, that sunlit day, and he didn't mention what he had seen, being sober-headed. Some time later, we were told by the landlady at a local inn, a woman saw the same sight, and when the young man heard this, he felt able to tell of his own experience without fear of being labelled a dreamer.

It is not surprising that ghosts should walk the Chase. It has seen more history than most areas, was for centuries the preserve of kings. William I gave it to his queen; later King John visited the Chase many times. The Larmer Tree which stood near Tollard Royal was said to be the point from which he summoned his huntsmen, and here medieval Chase courts were held. King John's House (of later than his day but built round an old hunting lodge) stands next to Tollard Royal church. Here too, the woods are thick and enclosing; small thatched cottages cling to the sides of the hollows below the down.

In later ages, lordship of the Chase passed to landowners such as the Earls of Pembroke and Salisbury, and finally to the Pitt-Rivers family. The Chase was disenfranchised in the nineteenth century, returning to individual landlords the rights over their woods and fences. Not before time, since it had long been a hotbed of poachers and smugglers. The bloody affrays between deer-stealers and keepers, the use of cross-bows, staves, nets and greyhounds, as well as guns, to kill deer, particularly from the sixteenth and seventeenth centuries onwards, are part of the legendary but true annals of the region. The original Larmer Tree is dead now, but a ghostly hunting horn is sometimes heard. Round the tree, in the late nineteenth century, General Pitt-Rivers, the father of scientific archaeology and first Inspector of Ancient Monuments, built pleasure gardens. Here people could come for a day out and to visit, free of charge, King John's House and the local museum at Farnham. General Pitt-Rivers even provided knives and forks, chairs, crockery and cooking stoves for the picnickers. (His collections are now housed in the Pitt-Rivers Museum at Oxford and other museums.)

After the disenfranchisement of the Chase, the fox, rather than deer, increasingly became the quarry of the hunt, since Englishmen, it seemed, had to hunt something.

> The story is told of the foreigner who stayed at a country-house where every morning the men of the party exclaimed: 'Tis a fine day! Let's go out and kill something. . .' Many Englishmen of fortune seem to suppose they are sent into this world to hunt foxes and shoot grouse and deer . . . the sessions of Parliament cannot be held till the frost is out of the ground and the foxes begin to breed.

So wrote the American Consul General in London, Adam Badeau, in 1886.[11]

Fox-hunting had become increasingly fashionable since the eighteenth century. In Sussex, in the Charlton country of the West Sussex downs, the first fox-hunt to be formed in England, the Charlton, had already become famous by then and the area was for a long time the headquarters of British hunting. The Duke of Monmouth, another son of Charles II, and so half-brother to the first Duke of Richmond, hunted with the Charlton, and promised that 'when he was King he would come and keep his Court at Charlton'.

The first Duke of Richmond bought Goodwood in 1687 as a hunting lodge, and in 1730 the second Duke built Fox Hall at East Dean as a lodge and banqueting room, where 'Charlton Pie' was eaten. Ladies assembled to watch the hunt, and in their day King William III and the Grand Duke of Tuscany also witnessed a 'fox-chase'. (In the Prince Regent's day, the fourth Duke of Richmond gave his pack to the Regent. In 1821 the pack had to be destroyed because the hounds showed symptoms of hydrophobia. Rabies was a much more common disease then. The fourth Duke of Richmond himself, while in Canada in 1818, separated a fighting pet fox and a dog, and contracted this disease, from which he died. Cures in hound books tended to recommend mixtures of rue, red sage, a handful of ground liverwort, with other unlikely ingredients such as scraped pewter and strong ale.)

In 1738 a celebrated ten-hour hunt took place, beginning at 7.45 am and ending at 5.50 pm. Earls, dukes, lords were among the field; casualties were many as the pack followed a vixen over hill and down dale, to a kill by the Arun. The huntsman was the legendary Tom Johnson, to whom a memorial was erected in Singleton church by the then Duke.

Deaf is that Ear which caught the opening Sound,
Dumb is that Tongue, which cheered the Hills around. . . .

Another vaunted exploit was that of the fifth Duke, who as a young man rode down one of the steepest parts of Bow Hill, near Goodwood.

Stubbs's three large paintings at Goodwood House are masterpieces which illustrate sporting events in the area. Painted while he was staying at Goodwood in 1759–60, one shows the third Duke with his wife and sister-in-law in the old costume of the Charlton Hunt watching racehorses training on the downs; another the Duke's brother-in-law shooting at Goodwood with Lord Holland; and the third the Duke hunting with his brother Lord George Lennox. In this painting Stubbs has included Halnaker windmill, and in the first, the harmonious and classical view that one

Goodwood racecourse

can still see from the top of the Trundle looking towards Chichester, with the silver curl of the Lavant, the inlets and harbour, and, rising from the sea, the faint outline of the downs of the Isle of Wight. Stubbs has also included Boxgrove Priory in his ideal scene, transposing its site to add to his brilliant evocation of a verdant countryside, a gilded sporting moment.

In the same hall at Goodwood is John Skeaping's sculpture of a racehorse with Lester Piggott up. Elisabeth Frink's superb life-size bronze horse stands to the west of the new grandstand at Goodwood Racecourse, its head silhouetted against the downs. The new stand was opened during 'Glorious Goodwood' of July 1980, but although racing at Goodwood still has great panache and is attended by royalty (and many others, even more so because there is a free view of the course from the Trundle), some are nostalgic for the grandstand of Edwardian days, which left space for a greater number of marquees round the beech trees which then lined the course more thickly, and of which Queen Alexandra was particularly fond. In a letter to the sixth Duke of Richmond in 1886, she thanked him for always making 'our annual stay at Goodwood the pleasantest week in the year'.[12] (She also had alterations made to the Royal Box so that it overlooked the wood and picnickers under the trees. The King and Queen each had a 'Pavilion' furnished with details such as mahogany seats, silver-plated flushing-handles, and monogrammed marble.)

The July meeting was at that time even more fashionable than Epsom or Ascot, and the neighbouring towns of Chichester and Bognor benefited in accommodating visitors. There had been racing at Goodwood since 1801; the third Duke established the first official meeting in 1802. The zenith of racing there was 1845, under the fifth Duke, with Lord George Cavendish Bentinck, the inventor of the horse-box. It was usual for horses to walk to meetings, as the great Priam did in 1830, walking from Newmarket to Epsom before winning the Derby. Bentinck sent a horse called Elis (descended from Priam) to Doncaster for the St Leger in his contraption like a gipsy caravan, and as the bookies knew the horse was still at Goodwood four days before the race, and knew nothing of the box, odds of 12 to 1 were laid against Elis, giving Bentinck a win of £12,000.

Bentinck trained for Richmond, making the Goodwood racing stables the best in the country, having a supremacy over rivals that has probably never been equalled; part of his success was due to the fact that he cleared woodland to make the famous Halnaker Gallops, that were protected by trees and laid with mould so that they were never unusable because of frost or snow.

Racecourses on the downs excel because of their springy turf, which dries quickly. Jockeys at Brighton Races will comment on the good going, even when meetings elsewhere have been cancelled. There has been racing on the downs at Brighton since 1770 – at Lewes even earlier, while on the downs near Salisbury there was mention of races in the 1600s.

The White Hawk course at Brighton was established in 1783, principally for officers of the Militia Regiments, and was patronised by the Prince of Wales the following year. The course is thought to have covered about two miles of the same horseshoe-shaped ridge that it does at present, marked by clearing away the furze. The view from the start today towards the coast eastwards has changed little since the Regent's day (Roedean is hardly an eyesore); furze clumps cluster at the rails and run in a triangle of golden orange northwards up Hogtrough Bottom above Bevendean to Falmer Hill. Only to the immediate west do the buildings of Whitehawk obtrude – the 'short grey grass sloping down by the bungalow houses to the sea', described in the 1930s by Graham Greene in *Brighton Rock*, with the gipsy children chasing rabbits, old bookies' tickets rotting into the chalk, 'the brilliant sky, the dust over the course, the torn betting cards and the short grass towards the dark sea beneath the down,' and as they close in on the Boy with their razors, the sun 'slanting low down over the downs from Shoreham'.

The inimitable mixture of glitter and dust that hangs about a racecourse. That one associates perhaps with the Derby above all other races. Since the late sixteenth and early seventeenth centuries, gentlemen of the court and country owners had been racing horses on the Epsom downs, meeting for a few days or a week or two. In the eighteenth century race meetings grew in importance. (The racing calendar was started in 1727.) By the end of the century the Derby was a national event. The grassy arena, with surrounding bosky trees, is an unrivalled setting. In the copse opposite the grandstand are blackthorn, wild apple and pear, hazel, elders, wych elm, wayfaring trees, larch and birch. The race-day crowds have been so often, and so well depicted. By William Frith in 'Derby Day', by Alfred Hunt, and Aaron Green, whose 'Epsom Downs' of 1863, with crinolined picnickers cutting into hams and raising glasses, while ragged urchins look on, is matched by the Frenchman Taine's description of a year earlier.

Brighton races

Le Derby is a vast green plain, rather hilly . . . over to the right, a line of great trees, with beyond them the green merging into blue hills . . . the most astonishing collection of cabs, coaches, droskis, four-in-hands, bearing cold meats, pâté, melons, fruit, wine and above all champagne . . . it is painful to see the poor . . . nearly all looking like starving dogs. . . . And the reason for this national passion for horses and racing, seems to me to be that . . . in a muddy country, one can only get about comfortably on horseback; their temperament calls for much physical exercise; all these customs have their climax in the Derby, which is their special celebration. . . . Today, anything is permitted: it is a release after a year of constraint.[13]

The Derby seldom changes, does not lose its brilliance. In a country where the German poet Heine saw jockeys whipping bystanders out of the way, and another foreigner commented, 'thousands follow the horses with as much uproar as if the Turkish cavalry were attacking',[14] it is not surprising that as the champagne fountained skywards for the 1981 Derby (won by the Aga Khan's Shergar), as the awnings of marquees fluttered under the gentle trees, as top-hats were raised and the open boots of Rolls Royces displayed their hampers, a group of revellers replied when questioned on hard times: 'What recession?'

The downs are as famous for racing stables as for racecourses. In an area such as that around Lambourn, where the downs are flat and elongated, the main features of the scenery, alongside clumps of beeches, are white rails and furlong marks. The clean, springy turf is ideal for training gallops.

In Sussex, one area where there are no fewer than four stables is Findon, under Cissbury Ring. And particularly renowned is Josh Gifford's stable, which in 1981 welcomed back Bob Champion and Aldaniti after their supreme Grand National triumph, a triumph of human courage, no less than a racing triumph, made possible also by the loyalty and commitment of the stables and its owner. It is a lucky stable, which under Bob Gore trained three Grand National winners, under Ryan Price, one National winner, and under its present owner one to date. It is the 'thrill of having a winner', which as Josh Gifford says, is the spur, and he himself was, as he modestly puts it, 'lucky enough to ride a lot of winners and see success that way', also. In fact he rode 700 winners, including those of the Topham Chase (twice), Schweppes Gold Trophy (four times) and Whitbread Gold Cup. He was Champion Jockey four times. Since then, as a trainer, he has had nearly 600 winners in eleven years.

Morale at the stable is kept high by success. (5 per cent of prize money also goes into the pool.) It offsets the hard work, and daily routine. The first string of horses is ridden out at 6.30 am. There are three types of

Racing plates and shoes, Josh Gifford's stables

Josh Gifford's training stables, Findon

gallops: the quick-draining downland turf that is seldom unusable; all-weather gallops of wood chippings; and sand. The downland hills are also valuable for building muscle. Beyond the gallops, flints can be a hazard for horses on the high downs; the stable has its own blacksmith, the sets of aluminium plates – front plates for racing, with light steel for the back plates – and everyday steel shoes, hanging in neat rows beside the chalked-up name of each horse. The care and detail, traditional tasks and tenacity, which lead up to the unrivalled moment at the finish. A moment which a village such as Findon toasts with pride.

Other sports, of the past – such as bull-baiting and cock-fighting – had their place in downland villages. Even a small village such as Rottingdean would have its regular bull-baits (at the King of Prussia pub) in the 1750s. There was also a cruel early sport called 'Throwing at Cocks', in which a cock was tied to a stake and pelted with bats or sticks, and an advanced version of this, 'Cock in the Pot', was played in the narrow lanes of Brighton. A rope was stretched between windows, and aim was taken at the cock in an earthen vessel suspended from the rope until the pot broke. It is difficult to believe today that this game was still popular until about 1780. (At least 150 years after the first game of cricket was played.)

It is thought that cricket, or a primitive form of it, was in fact played centuries before the first recorded game. Shepherds holding 'criccs' in their hands are shown in a thirteenth-century mural in Cocking church, by the South Downs. These criccs are like hockey sticks, or the early, curved, cricket bats, and the figures holding them in the wall painting are in local, thirteenth-century dress. Shepherds may have played cricket with these bats, and stones, on the slopes of the downs from very early times.

The first reference to the game is to schoolboys playing cricket in Guildford, but the first recorded game as such was at Boxgrove Priory in 1622. The game was played in the churchyard, among the tombstones (two churchwardens being among the players). Two or three other games were recorded during that century, and all were in Sussex. From the early eighteenth century cricket was played increasingly and in other areas, but it was in the triangle formed by Arundel, Chichester and Midhurst that the foundations of modern cricket were laid. At Slindon was born, and is buried, Richard Newland, the 'Father of Cricket', captain of Slindon and captain of England, whose nephew Richard Nyren handed on the skills to the Hambledon eleven, who played first on Broadhalfpenny Down, and who made Hambledon as great in the 1750s and 1760s as Slindon had been in the 1730s and 1740s.

Other great champions in the early days were the second Duke of Richmond, and Sir William Gage of Firle. It is likely that the Duke had the edge over his rival, as he employed good cricketers as grooms and

gardeners for his team. He was responsible for drawing up the first known Laws, before two matches which took place in 1727, against a Surrey team. In 1728 his team was playing Sir William Gage's at Lewes, and in that same year the first county game was played – Sussex versus Kent.

It was a Petersfield man, John Small, who played for Hambledon, and was also a skater, huntsman and violinist, who introduced the straight bat in 1775, and who scored the first recorded century. He played until he was 61. 'Esteemed a very excellent player with great condescension and affability', was the Prince of Wales (George IV), whose present to Brighton of a cricket ground became the first real county ground.[15]

Other celebrated figures of these early cricketing regions are many. The fourth Duke of Richmond, who founded the MCC, of whom there is a charming portrait as a boy, with three of the curved bats, at Goodwood.

William Lillywhite, the 'Sussex nonpareil', whose father managed two brickfields at Goodwood, and who himself later moved to Brighton. He said of his play, 'I bowl the best ball in England', and he championed the round-arm bowling which was at first considered 'foul' by the 'Noblemen and Gentlemen of the Mary-le-bone Club'. (It was said to have been invented by a girl in Kent, whose full skirts prevented her bowling underarm.) Lillywhite always wore top hat, Gladstone collar, dark cravat and wide cotton braces, and saw no reason to change with the times.

Tom Box, John Wisden of the *Cricketers' Almanack*, countless others leading up to the age of Ranji and Fry. Hove was another of the famous grounds, where W. G. Grace often played. Originally the Hove ground was the Old Brunswick, opened in 1841. Grace described the pitch as 'beachy'. He scored 170 and 56, not out, there when he was 16 in 1864, and in the last match at the old ground in 1871, for John Lillywhite's benefit, 217. (It was not there, but at Warnham Lodge, that the most likeable cricket story was born. Mead, the Essex bowler, won fame there for bowling a ball through Grace's beard: 'Sorry, doctor, she slipped.') John Arlott has said of Hove that it is 'pre-eminently the southern England cricket ground. It could not be anywhere else in the world; and for many Englishmen overseas it is a nostalgic memory. . . .'[16]

During the Victorian and Edwardian eras, country-house matches became part of the fashionable scene. Downland mansions in their parks, still, but more democratically, furnish settings which are as much part of the English tradition as village green cricket played in such villages as Findon, which have a long history of the game. Perhaps the old days of cricketing landlords, of teams travelling in hired brakes or the grocer's van, of roast duck and beef-and-pickle lunches, and beer at twopence a pint, have gone for ever, but the sight of players in their flannels on a fine expanse of turf under the smiling green hills, as the shadows lengthen under the trees, is what many people inwardly see when they conjure up an English summer Sunday.

5

. . . the flock in woolly fold . . .

John Keats

AGRICULTURE AND FARM LIFE · SHEPHERDS · COUNTRY INDUSTRIES

W. H. Hudson, that great writer on the English countryside, stated at the beginning of this century that if he had unlimited wealth, he would like to own a downland hill in Sussex, to place on it, as a gift to posterity, an over-life-size representation of six great black oxen drawing a harvest wagon, with labourers tossing up the sheaves. 'To begin with, a sculptor of genius would be required, a giant among artists; and the materials would be gigantic blocks of granite and marble – red, black, grey and yellow. . . .'[1]

Sad that his vision has never taken shape, to place oxen, as Elisabeth Frink's sculpture has placed the horse, emblematically in their setting and in our conscious memory. For as Hudson surmised they would be, draught oxen are creatures of the past – the black, and the red, which were the old Sussex breed. They stalk like heavy shadows across the fields of history, and like other farming traditions which endure longer and go back farther than those of more brittle industries, are regarded with affection and turned to for reassurance by even those who have never been within yards of a tractor or turnip field. One can't, without a feeling of nostalgia, read that in 1912 the *West Sussex Gazette* recorded the sale of probably the last two pairs of plough oxen in the area to come up for a bid – Frost and Fairman, and Rock and Ruby.

One or two teams lingered on, at places such as Exceat on the Cuckmere, partly for display. They had been more than twice as numerous as draught horses. Now in some areas (Chiddingly for instance), shire horses are again being trained for use because of the cost of fuel. But the oxen, alas, are gone.

Interior of coppice-worker's hut, Clapham Wood

99

Farmers used to be drawn to burial in a farm wagon, by a slow team of oxen.

The years like great black oxen tread the world,
And God the herdsman goads them on behind. . . .[2]

We miss the shepherd on the downs, the sheep-dipping in many-coloured dyes, the smell of hayricks in the sun, the harvest cart with its straw catching in the hedges of a narrow lane, the milk churns stood under the dappled shade of a tree on their wooden platform, like one near Askerswell in Dorset which is so mossed over, so interwoven with tree roots, so gnarled itself, that it is embedded in the landscape.

In Worthing Museum, there is a room-setting labelled 'downland kitchen'. I look at it in amazement, because it is the Dorset farmhouse kitchen in which I spent part of my childhood, with its kitchen range, stone

Milk churn stand, Askerswell

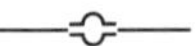

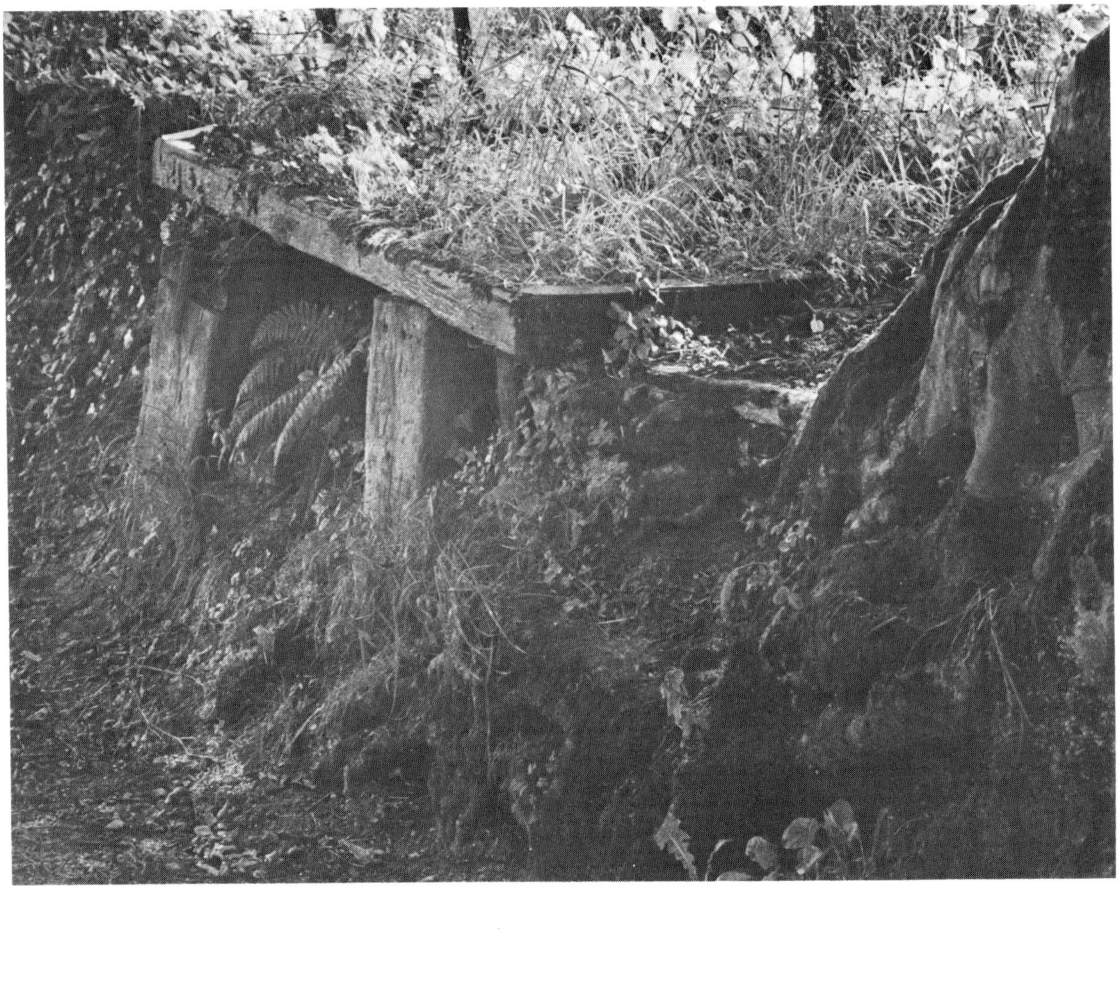

copper, wooden ceiling-rack for clothes-drying, oil lamps, bread oven, stone floor. From there we walked, when in need of supplies not brought by the travelling grocer's van, to neighbouring farms where children's shouts announced a pig killing, or through a yard filled with pied guinea fowl and bantams to a dairy where the round pounds of butter glistened with drops of water, muslin was draped over pans of cream, eggs rested on beds of straw. There was no need, there still seems no need to me, for plastic containers, electric mixers, pile carpets.

Innovations in farming have always been practical, however, in their day, and undoubtedly it is because so many farm tools have been immensely practical that they have been used for so long. (Bill-hooks, swap-hooks, dibbles. The sickle, for instance, one of the most ancient tools, was used in some places for hand-reaping until the end of the last century.)

Development has gone in cycles. Much of downland is now under the plough, but not so much as in the Napoleonic era, and in places not so much as in Roman times. Sheep and cattle are being grazed in leys (temporary pasture, later ploughed for arable), which enrich the soil, perhaps after years of repeated crop growing, but the animals are possibly not so intensively used as in the days of mid-Victorian 'high farming', when every conceivable method besides direct fertilisation was used to put back into the soil what was taken out, in an almost factory-like process for obtaining high yields. Without cheap labour to move hurdles (electric fences are now a modern alternative), sheep in particular cannot be used so easily to clear ground and manure it at the same time, as did the 'golden hoof' flocks of the past.

'The more prosperous farming is, the farther up the hill it goes,' explains Mr Dick Passmore of Church Farm, Coombes in Sussex. 'When it's not prosperous it comes down into the plain.' And he can see, in a very steep field on the down, not now ploughed, furrows running at an angle up the hill, which was the way in which such a difficult field would have been ploughed, at a date in the last century when corn was at a premium.

In 1900 much land was returned to pasture, but during the 1914–18 war it was again ploughed; then it 'fell down' between the wars, but during the Second World War, land at Coombes that was not part of the army training area was again used for arable. Today all but the steepest land is at times ploughed. (Between 1939 and 1944, the area of the United Kingdom under the plough increased from 12,000,000 to 19,400,000 acres and the output of food by 70 per cent. Sussex, for instance, more than doubled its arable acreage.)

This is typical of the agricultural history of the downs – this and the fertility, or at times exhaustion, of the light, chalky downland soil. Highly skilled husbandry is needed on a downland farm. After years of cultivation, Neolithic and Iron Age peoples had to move their farm sites in order to tap new ground, and it must have been one of the more fearful mysteries of their darker ages as to why the fruitfulness of the land should suddenly fail them.

The farm at Coombes, on the South Downs, is a perfect example of a downland farm, not least because of its site in its hamlet of two or three houses in a cluster in the coomb, with a church of flint rubble, approached through a field where sheep, geese and horses nudge the churchgoer.

At the time of the Domesday Survey in 1086, including the lord's land there was 'land for eight ploughs' at Coombes, with twenty-seven villagers and four smallholders; a church; woodland with four pigs; and salt pans. (By comparison there was land at Bristelmestune (Brighton) for only three ploughs, with eighteen villagers and nine smallholders; while at Shoreham (Soresha) there was land for fifteen ploughs, with twenty-six villagers and forty-nine smallholders, and woodland with forty pigs.)[3]

The salt pans were in the saltings or marshes in the Adur Valley beside the farm. When the tidal Adur was low, the water evaporated to leave the valuable mineral. Traces of the pans can be seen in the area, now drained and very fertile. (The saltings are shown on an exceptional 1677 map at the farm, as are also some narrow field strips and the starting post for early 'letter races' along the post route to Findon. Names remain the same – Snow Hill, Ox Brook, the Croft, the Ham.) The coastal plain of West Sussex is a very fertile area, with some of the highest yields of wheat and barley coming from the strip between Worthing and the Hampshire border.

The upland soil at Coombes, as elsewhere on the downs, is relatively shallow. Stock get water from tanks, and from a working dewpond. (At one time the government ordered dewponds to be filled in, as they were thought to harbour disease, but now the policy has been reversed.)

'To a thinking mind few phenomena are more strange than the state of little ponds on the summits of chalk hills,' observed Gilbert White, describing those above his house at Selborne; and on the Berkshire Downs he measured with notched sticks a rise of an inch or two of water in a pond, though no rain fell. The explanation was dense fog.

Dewponds, or mist ponds may, some people still believe, have been used by prehistoric man. But certainly an Anglo-Saxon charter of the ninth century refers to Orna Mere dewpond on the Wiltshire downs, so by that date the procedure was known.

A dewpond was made by digging a shallow basin in the chalk, which was lined with flint and rubble. Then came a layer of straw, on to which sheep would be turned, to tread it down. Then followed a clay layer, which would again be well puddled by sheep or oxen. Soot or lime could be added to the layers to prevent insects and worms boring through. Rain filled the ponds, and they were kept full by the sea-mists or other mists, which are so common in downland, especially in summer on hot mornings or evenings. On a hot still evening you can see the drops of moisture

condensing in the cool air above the water of a pond, then dropping as dew on to the surface. Cement would be used instead of clay today, but the straw layer would still provide insulation, to keep the pond area cold. Old ponds can be seen on the tops of many downs; some are wired off, and hold water which becomes covered with flowering weed when there are no sheep to keep the edges puddled and clean.

Besides sheep at Coombes (for fat lambs as well as wool), which run on the downland pasture, beef cattle are kept. A fold is built in a field for lambing, with individual pens, under the care of a shepherd. The breeding flock of sheep are Welsh half-bred ewes; the rams are Kerrys, Suffolk or Dorset Down (Dorset Downs are much in demand at present). A Dutch Texal ram has also been introduced. These rams are chosen to produce a good meaty type of lamb for market. The Southdown sheep has become rarer now, because people choose lean meat, and the Southdown was a small breed, fat and with a delicious flavour. (It also produces good early lambs.) But breeders are now trying to enlarge it. At one time shepherds would complain they were no bigger than mice.

103

It was the wild thyme in the downland turf that was said to give Southdown mutton its celebrated flavour. The true downland turf that is becoming rare now. It evolved over centuries, trodden and nibbled close by sheep, followed by rabbits. Dominated by fescue grasses, with short herbs and creeping plants such as thyme and rock rose – which don't mind the alkaline, nutrient-deficient soil where taller plants grow with difficulty. 'In a space of one square foot of ground,' wrote Hudson in *Nature in Downland*, 'a dozen or twenty or more species of plants may be counted, and on turning up a piece of turf the innumerable fibrous interwoven roots have the appearance of cocoa-nut matting. It is indeed this thick layer of interlaced fibres that gives the turf its springiness, and makes it so delightful to walk upon. It is fragrant too. The air, especially in the evening of a hot spring day, is full of a fresh herby smell, to which many minute aromatic plants contribute. . . .'

Where sheep no longer graze the turf, and since the advent of myxomatosis, which decimated the rabbit population, taller grasses and plants have grown up, followed by bushes and scrub; later, on patches of deeper soil, trees may take root. Even where the downs have not been ploughed, they are in danger of losing their well-loved character.

But the steepest flanks, as at Coombes, where grazed, keep their smooth roundness. At Church Farm, too, conservation has long been practised. 'Farmers are country people and therefore we like to see everything around us,' says Mr Passmore. 'We have tried in our own way to make sure there's no ungainly development.' Long before it became conservation policy to protect habitats for wildlife, he had his 'follies' or clumps of trees where pheasants and other birds could find cover. Recently four thousand trees have been planted in strips up two down sides, and a plantation on a hill top. ('These hills are my first love,' Mr Passmore says. On flat land he feels claustrophobic.) On the verges of tracks, cowslips and other threatened species run riot, to give added value to the Farm Tours which Jenny Passmore at Church Farm has initiated. (And which are enjoyed by about a hundred groups – three to five thousand people – a year. Having studied farming in Denmark as well as at home, she is well equipped to give children in particular an insight into farming and the countryside – education being perhaps our best long-term hope of achieving true conservation.)

Many problems between farmers or landowners and the public being far from new. 'Their land is threaded with paths which invite the walker...,' wrote John Burroughs in 1883 of the English. 'I heard of a surly nobleman near London who took it into his head to close a foot-path. ... The pedestrians objected ... the aristocrat was beaten.'[4]

'Footpaths were originally created for people going to work,' a young farmer pointed out to me. 'I can't run after people who leave gates open or trample crops – I have no hope of prosecuting them.' Ramblers are equally hot-tongued about farmers who plough up paths without reinstating them. When the public can be better trusted, perhaps the question will become less vexed. Meanwhile, as a farmer remarked with a laugh, 'Under the new law [Wildlife and Countryside Act], I'll be able to let my beef bulls roam.' A cow with a calf is far more dangerous, or a dairy bull. The public will have to know its bulls.

'Sussex is not so good for sheep,' we were told by a shepherd in Cranborne Chase, 'because of dogs.'

In any locality near an urban area, there is a problem with stray, or badly trained dogs, which may chase sheep. On the other hand, this shepherd told us that sheep in all districts were 'coming back'. 'They come and go,' over the years, but at present when the price of lamb is high, they can be profitable. Sheep don't need such a big outlay of capital as some farming enterprises; a flock can be bought quickly, then sold later; large buildings do not have to be built.

Many of the old breeds of sheep have died out – but some survive. On Fontmell Down, where the Dorset Naturalists' Trust owns land, and where the National Trust also has land (which can be walked over and which is a memorial to Thomas Hardy), there are some Dorset Horns. Dorset Horn rams, in particular, with their intricately curling horns, look truly ancient. A lovely stretch of downland, its flanks, beyond a cross-dyke, fall away covered with furze and wild rose bushes. From the private nature trust land the smell of fragrant orchids floats on the wind.

Although they can lamb three times in two years, Dorset Horns are not very numerous nowadays, and need 'a lot of shepherding', because their horns can easily catch in wire or fences. (Poll Dorset are popular as crossing rams; the Dorset Down took over in Sussex when the Southdown became too small – now Suffolks, which originated from a cross between the Southdown and Norfolk, are also popular.) The Norfolk Horn, Wiltshire Horn and Berkshire Knot have in the main died out, although some specialist flocks such as Wiltshire Horns have been reintroduced in their native county and elsewhere. Wiltshire Horns once flourished on Salisbury Plain and the high downland. Many of the early breeds were long, goat-like sheep with mediocre yields of wool but giving good mutton

Dorset Horn ram, with ewes

(the Southdown was an early example of sheep bred to be stocky and hornless, with a high-quality fleece as well as good flavour). The earliest domesticated sheep of all, of which remains have been found in excavated middens, resembled a Soay ram, with very heavy curved horns.

In the same way one can trace back to Neolithic origins, breeds of cattle, such as the Sussex. As well as sheep, pigs, dogs and goats, Neolithic farmers had domesticated oxen, as opposed to the giant wild ox. The dark red Sussex cattle are descended from the red Sussex oxen; the modern Sussex is in demand for cross-breeding (is even used in France to breed in improved flavour to beef). In his day, Defoe remarked on Sussex bullocks, and mentioned Sir John Fagg of Steyning's bullocks which weighed *80 stone a quarter* when killed at Smithfield.

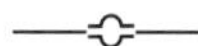

'Between East Bourne and Steyning, which is thirty-three miles, the Downs are about six miles wide, and in this tract there are about 200,000 ewes kept; the whole tract of the Downs in their full extent, is stocked with sheep, and the amazing number they keep, is one of the most singular circumstances in the husbandry of England.' So wrote the Rev. Arthur Young in his *General View of the Agriculture of the County of Sussex*, in 1813. But although John Ellman, who farmed at Glynde, was then perfecting the Southdown breed, which was an economic feeder (the downland pasture made its wool fine – rich food was said to make wool coarser), the number of sheep on the downs was not new. In 1341, 110,000 sheep were recorded in Sussex (which is roughly equivalent to the number in 1944, although in 1939 there were nearly 230,000). In 1724, Defoe estimated 600,000 within six miles of Dorchester (in Dorset as a whole, 500,000 in 1850; 100,000 in 1959; 106,609 in 1965. While farther back the Domesday Survey records 800 sheep at Ashmore, over 1000 at Cranborne and 1600 at Puddletown).

Leonard Mascall, whose *The Governmente of Cattell* was published in 1587, and who was thought to have lived at Plumpton Manor near Lewes, describes how sheep were fed on grass and in winter with hay and tares, eked out with elm, ash and other leaves called 'browse', also barley straw and peas haulm. Vast sheep walks being the main feature of the downs from the early Middle Ages onwards, it was wool which was the most prized product of the sheep, and which provided England's staple export. 'This nation is the most famous for the great quantity of wool of any in the world,' wrote Aubrey in the seventeenth century, and he added that Wiltshire was the county with the most sheep and wool. Raw wool was the original export, but the cloth trade, after a period of decline, was stimulated by government action (more ruthless than in our day) in the reigns of Edward II and Edward III (imported cloth was prohibited), and from then on was the most important English manufacture until the industrial era: '. . . the cloth making is at *an end*,' stated Cobbett.

But sheep have often flourished on the downs in just those times when people have been in depressed circumstances. Enclosure in the sixteenth century, when wool was profitable, caused villages to be depopulated; again in the eighteenth century, parliamentary enclosures worked against small landowners rather than large (enclosures in Sussex were made 'from the earliest antiquity', so little parliamentary enclosure ensued there); in the depressed 1930s, the downs were alive with flocks. Particularly in a county such as Wiltshire, deserted villages can be found on the downs. Snap, to the west of Aldbourne, was a village that was cleared to make way for sheep as late as the nineteenth century.

This recurrent rough treatment of people must have been all the more harsh as common grazing land became less and less. By comparison, the manorial system of the early Middle Ages seems more democratic, in spite of the feudal lords of the manor, to whom the villagers owed tithes. They had to work on the lord's demesne or home farm, but were allowed the produce from small strips of land, while a few freeholders also owned strips by right. The bundles or scattered strips were in open or common fields. Here animals could be grazed after the crops were gathered, while even in the sixteenth century and later one finds tenants being allowed to keep sheep on the 'lord's down' at certain times of the year.

Medieval strips were of varying sizes, often about half an acre, and usually a furlong (furrow-long) long. The land was divided by 'balks' of turf, and pieces of unused land were called 'No man's land' or 'Jack's land'. The balks became footpaths and roadways. Ploughing was done in a co-operative manner. On hillsides the plough would be taken horizontally along the hill and the sods turned downhill, with the plough then returning idle. The grassy balks prevented the furrows sliding into the next parcel of land, but gradually the soil would pile up against the banks or balks so that terraces were formed, separated by the lynchets.

(Lynchet is a vexed term. Lynches, linces or links are other variations, and the word is often applied to the terrace itself. They can clearly be seen on many downs – at Abbotsbury, at Sherrington in the Wylye Valley, Mere, Winterbourne Steepleton, countless other places. Many are difficult to date. The squarer terraces or fields, of an earlier, probably Celtic date, may more safely be called, as W. G. Hoskins has pointed out, 'ancient field system'. Flints raked off the ground often made the ridges which surround the squares – and which can be faintly seen, especially from the air. A good example was named 'The Bible', in Bible Bottom in South Malling in Sussex. Two rectangular strips enclosed by raised banks, resembling an open Bible, were divided by a path or roadway, making the hinge or fold of the book.

The principle by which 'strip lynchets' were formed is logical enough. As a present-day farmer pointed out, wherever you have a fence, you will tend to get a 'drop' which will become a ridge later. Any division, whether balk, bank or hedge, will accumulate its own soil, leaving a mound even if the hedge is later grubbed up or the balk ploughed over. Some of the terraces were also likely to have been purposely constructed, to make cultivation easier.)

By the sixteenth century, 'up and down' farming was in practice – an early form of ley farming or mixed husbandry, with corn yields increasing, and more stock kept. A technique of floating the water-meadows was also introduced to improve fodder. By the next century, clover was much in use, and the phrase to be 'in clover' became proverbial. Sainfoin (which is particularly suited to chalk soil), rape, lucerne and turnips were also established. The eighteenth century was the great century of innovation and improvements in agriculture as elsewhere, and by the time Arthur Young was writing his book, landowners and farmers were undertaking the most diverse schemes of land drainage and breeding:

'The greatest improvement that I know undertaken in this county, has been effected on the Stag-park at Petworth, some years ago, by the Earl of Egremont . . . and every part of the park has been since drained in the most effectual manner. . . .' (The Earl was a great innovator, who even cultivated rhubarb and opium for medicinal uses.)

Field systems, near Cerne Abbas

'Mr Ellman cuts off the tails of his lambs at the time of castration. . . .

'In Adfriston parish, six acres of coleseed and eight or nine ton of hay, are used for 450 sheep, with the Down.

'. . . it would be a neglect not to describe the quickset-hedges at Goodwood, which are very capital, and trained in a most masterly manner. The Duke of Richmond planted them. . . .

'A practice which Mr Thomas Ellman adopts at Shoreham, is that of breaking up his layers (clover, ray and trefoil) for summer-tares and rape. . . .'

It is not clear whether it was this Mr Ellman, or his more famous relation at Glynde, who provided a harvest supper of 16 stone of beef, 8 stone of mutton, 1 cwt of plum pudding, 50 gallons of beer, bread and cheese. ('The origin of this custom is thought by Mr Ellman to be this: that when labour was scarce, the neighbouring artisans assisted the farmers in their harvest for two or three days, gratis; and the harvest-home was a recompense for it.')

There seemed little enough recompense for labourers. In a year, in the early nineteenth century, a labourer in Sussex might earn £27 2s, of which 9s would be an extra at haymaking time but an equal 9s would be lost through bad weather or 'slight illness'. His annual expenses would be £8 14s (including rent £2 10s; clothing: frock, waistcoat and breeches and two shirts – £1 1s; one pair of stout shoes, nailed 9s, a pair of stockings 4s; with in addition a gown and petticoat, two shifts and two aprons, two pairs of stockings and strong shoes, for his wife). Then came the price of food – so that for a family of six, a 'deficiency of earnings' of 6s 2d per annum was calculated, while for a family of eight, with some children earning, a deficiency of £14 2d was calculated.[5] Much thought was given by the serious minded to conditions in the poor house.

While the poor suffered from the Napoleonic wars with the rising price of corn, tenant farmers and landed gentry prospered, and could afford to make their improvements. When peace came the price of corn fell, many farmers were ruined; the protective Corn Law of 1815 sought to adjust the balance, but made conditions harsher for the oppressed, in town or country. In the rural south, bad corn and beer might be given in lieu of wages.

'Pelling could tell tales of hard times. He was probably a ploughboy at seven or eight years old. He had never missed a day's work in his life . . . had known what it was to start work with no better breakfast than a cold raw turnip! It was the knowledge of such sufferings of the many which made my father into one of the few corn-growers who dared to stand with Cobden and Bright in the "hungry forties",' wrote Maude Robinson in *A South Down Farm in the Sixties*.[6]

But after the peak of agricultural prosperity in about 1870, corn too was to be doomed, if only for a while, through competition from abroad.

Into this state of decline, particularly felt in a county such as Dorset, where the rural population decreased rapidly as a consequence, and where there was little industry, dairying brought reprieve. Equally, in the farming depression of the later 1920s and 1930s, the open-air milking machine or bail invented by A. J. Hosier, at Wexcombe, near Wilton, was a revolutionary marvel. On the downs, the portable bail was of immense practical value. Enterprising farmers also forced and introduced water to upland areas, making it possible to keep cattle there. At present, with all its more modern methods, dairying is supreme on many downs in the western half of the country. Dorset is one of the most intensive dairying areas in the United Kingdom, if not in Europe.

On the eastern downs, such as those in Sussex, arable dominates; all the chalk downs are noted for barley, but wheat, oats and root crops can also do well.

'But the lads and the lasses to the sheep-shearing go. . . .'

The shepherd of the old days, that now semi-mythological character with his hut and sheep bells, has always seemed more independent than many other farm workers. According to the old system, he was paid some of his wages in kind, being given a few lambs which he was allowed to keep with his master's flock. He was in some respects in partnership with the farmer.

'In the future, it will be mostly contract shepherding,' is one (female) shepherd's opinion of current trends. 'Nothing fossilises, you know,' she wisely added. Pointing out also that 'it's a working community in a village', or should be. Cottage industries and small enterprises bring life, whereas retired people may tend to 'come down and mow their lawns and complain about the noise of small industries'. Shepherding, she feels, is a good outdoor life, and very enjoyable; more accessible to women than it used to be.

In the past, a shepherd's lonely and individual life seems to have bred a breed of thoughtful, often self-educated men. Samuel Pepys, as early as 1660, visiting the downs, remarked:

> Upon the Downs where a flock of sheep was, and the most pleasant and innocent sight I ever saw. We found a shepherd and his little boy reading, far from any houses or sight of people the Bible. . . . We took notice of his wollen knit stockings of two colours mixed, and his shoes shod with iron shoes both at toes and heels, and great nails in the soles of his feet. The Downes are full of stones. . . .

One of the most remarkable shepherds was John Dudeney, who was born at Plumpton in Sussex in 1782. His family had been shepherds for generations, and he started work when he was eight. His master allowed him to run a sheep with the flock, and he used the savings he made from its wool and from catching wheatears, to buy books. (A shepherd could make as much as fifty pounds between July and September by trapping wheatears in traps in runs in the ground, for sale to the Brighton poulterers.) 'I have sometimes been on the hills in winter from morning to night, and have not seen a single person during the whole day', Dudeney wrote in his reminiscences. '... I remember once, whilst with my father, the snow froze into ice on my eyelashes, and he breathed on my face to thaw it off.' (A sensation not unknown in present cold winters such as that of 1981/2, when snowdrifts up to several feet deep on many downs, even the mild South Downs, cut farmers off for days until an excavator could clear a path. A farmer in Cranborne Chase told us how he carried all his new-born lambs to cover, fighting against a blizzard, until his legs were frozen stiff and numb with cold.)

The shepherd Dudeney studied geography, astronomy and mathematics; taught himself French, and read the Bible in the original, having also

Shepherd's smock

taught himself Hebrew. He wanted a telescope to enjoy the wide sea and land views from the hills, but couldn't afford one, so found some old lenses and fitted them into a pasteboard case. All his books he buried at night under a large flintstone on the down, calling this his 'understone library'. In 1804 he gave up shepherding, taking a job in Baxter's printing works at Lewes, and later became a schoolmaster, and was a founder of the Mechanics' Institution in that town. He died aged 70, famed for his kindness.

Other shepherds of character are presented in Hudson's *A Shepherd's Life*, with tales of their dogs, of sheep-stealers, and of those hanged for the crime, when 'Hunger made the people reckless'; of gamekeepers, deer poachers, and of the desperate mobs who broke up the new farm machinery which was taking away their jobs – 'a great excited crowd in which men and cattle and sheep were mixed together in the wide street . . . and of shouting and noise of smashing machinery, and finally of the mob pouring forth over the down on its way to the next village. . . .' In these passages too, shepherds such as Isaac and Caleb Bawecombe of the south Wiltshire downs, seem a race apart. Caleb, who started work aged six, would still talk of shepherding when he was old and disabled:

> He was long miles away from his beloved home now, lying on his back, a disabled man who would never again follow a flock on the hills nor listen to the sounds he loved to hear – the multitudinous tremulous bleatings of the sheep, the tinklings of numerous bells, and crisp ringing bark of his dog. But his heart was there still, and the images of past scenes were more vivid in him than they can ever be in the minds of those who live in towns and read books. . . .
> . . . we were silent for a time, and then he uttered these impressive words: 'I don't say that I want to have my life again. . . . But if 'twas offered to me and I was told to choose my work, I'd say, Give me my Wiltsheer Downs again and let me be a shepherd there all my life long.'[7]

Even today, the spirit of the downs can get under a shepherd's skin. Laurie Skeats, flockmaster on Crichel Down in Dorset, is in charge of a flock of sixteen hundred sheep. (Scotch half-bred Suffolk cross ewes with Hampshire tups, producing good fat lambs. Texal rams and Mule sheep are also now popular in the Dorset area.) Laurie Skeats is filled with enthusiasm not only for shepherding, but for its history. He has a large collection of shepherding tools and memorabilia, which he exhibits at shows. He himself uses a leg crook for working every day (neck crooks were another variety, and there were also in the past special dipping crooks), and at lambing time in early March he uses traditional square lambing pens of hurdles topped by chestnut paling, with bales of straw (or more recently, with plastic roofing). He sleeps on the spot during lambing,

and says that many of the things he does for the sheep remain the same as when he worked as a boy with his father, also a shepherd.

A craftsman also, Laurie makes beautiful walking-sticks, and thumb-sticks with horn or antler forks. For exhibition purposes, he asked a needlewoman to make a traditional smock, copied from one in Dorchester Museum. Of unbleached linen, with self-colour smocking, it took 300 hours to make. Colours of working smocks varied from county to county – some were green, others grey, blue or black – but Sunday or special occasion smocks were usually white.

The old skills; the old love of place.

'It is', Laurie Skeats says, talking of his work and of that unsurpassed reach of countryside where his sheep graze, 'a second bit of paradise up there on Crichel Down.'

Nor can one forget that in the past, in good times or bad – and harsh times were not inevitably harsh for all – country life had its measured solace and seasonal joys. Shepherds and farmers, and villagers, had the high days and (few) holidays which mark so colourfully much of the literature of the last century, or anecdotes of those times. It is not sentimentality alone that makes the old country scene appear so brightly etched to us. How can a modern man lapped by central heating appreciate fully the changing seasons; feel as keenly in his marrow-bones the first sun of March? When he is bombarded by visual images, see with the same perception the first unfolding leaves, or, in November, a silver sickle of birds above the dark fields? And writers of those days are conveying impressions gained in a countryside so much less uniform and curtailed than that of today.

'. . . the quiet life was the usual thing for farmers in those days,' writes Maude Robinson of her Saddlescombe farm. '. . . the utterly quiet life on the Downs in winter, shut in by snow or rain, with no neighbours to associate with, no wireless, no gramophone. . . .' 'The paper did not reach the South Downs every day, only when a team went into Brighton taking hay or straw and bringing back a load of stable manure to coax the barren, chalky "layings" to produce a meagre crop of the then much desired wheat. . . .' 'Yet we were perfectly content and happy and never thought of our life as dull.'[8]

> *Here's the pink and the lily,*
> *And the daffydowndilly,*
> *To adorn and perfume the sweet meadows in June.*
> *'Tis all before the plough the fat oxen go slow;*
> *But the lads and the lasses to the sheep-shearing go.*[9]

The indoor games, the dancing round a maypole or in barns, the fairs and fairings, sheep-shearings and harvest homes, thread ebulliently through accounts of the past. They spark and glow in the pages of Thomas Hardy's novels and illumine a pastoral counterpart to the more sombre events of his Wessex. The chapter headings to a novel such as *Far From the Madding Crowd* provide a calendar of everyday and yet portentous happenings. 'The Fair – The Sheep-Washing – The Revel.'

'It was the first day of June, and the sheep-shearing season culminated, the landscape, even to the leanest pasture, being all health and colour. Every green was young, every pore was open, and every stalk was swollen with racing currents of juice. God was palpably present in the country, and the devil had gone with the world to town.

. . . In comparison with cities, Weatherbury was immutable. . . . Five decades hardly modified the cut of a gaiter, the embroidery of a smock-frock, by the breadth of a hair.

. . . So the barn was natural to the shearers, and the shearers were in harmony with the barn. . .'[10]

Fairs were held all over Wessex. One of the most famous was the annual cattle and horse fair at Toller Down. On the high downs between Warminster and Amesbury, was held the strange Yarnborough Castle fair, one of the most important sheep fairs in the country, when sheep for miles around were driven to the fair in the great prehistoric earthwork. In Sussex, Lewes was an important fair, rising to eminence in the late eighteenth and early nineteenth centuries, especially as the Southdown sheep became world-famous. By the late 1860s as many as 50,000 sheep were penned near the prison for the fair, of which there were many in all downland areas. Again in Sussex, the Findon fair, held since 1790 on Nepcote Green, is now the largest of its kind in Sussex and Surrey. In 1981 there were 8,500 sheep on the village green. A Southdown ram fetched £200. (The champion ram was from Gote Farm, Ringmer.) Sellers come from as far afield as Wales and Somerset; the sheep, since the mid-1920s, come in lorries. Horn and iron crooks are seen, or thumbsticks of hazel with ferrules of cut-down cartridge cases. An old shepherd will tell of the bells that were of use particularly in foggy weather, and of cutting yokes to hold these from yew wood while sitting on the downs.

Other village occupations important in downland areas were those of the miller, wheelwright and blacksmith. The village carpenter repaired farm wagons; the blacksmith also made the 'tips and taps', which were the men's shoe irons on which Pepys commented. Linen, until the advent of machine-made cotton cloth, was an important material, woven from locally grown flax, as at Ringmer in Sussex. A squire's inventory of 1605 lists many towels and table cloths, damask napkins with 'laice worke', and flaxen napkins; about ten pairs of sheets.

Brewing was, and is, a vital industry – with centres at places such as Lewes, Dorchester and Cerne Abbas, and in Kent. W. H. Hudson describes with uncustomary disgust the seventy public houses in Chichester in his day, where at eleven the 'drink-degraded wretches' stumbled into the night. 'These loathly human objects are strangely incongruous at that spot, under the great spire, in sight of the green open healthy downs, in perhaps the richest agricultural district in England.'[11] But by that time town life had begun to impinge on the countryside, had lured away the village men, and was no doubt in sharp contrast to the life and robuster drinking habits of earlier times on that same open down.

In villages and cottages, basket-making was another flourishing industry, still undertaken at places such as Abbotsbury. There were also the 'green men' who collected herbs to dry on racks in their homes; mole trappers; makers of sheep and horse bells and brasses; skilled flint knappers; pea-stick gatherers; (women) gleaners; saddlers. . . .

One of the earliest and most important trades was that of the coppice worker (from the French 'couper' to cut; introduced by the Normans), and one or two still exist. Hazel coppices were allowed to grow for anything up to fifteen or sixteen years ('Lord Pembroke's are kept till 20 years' – states an old Cranborne Chase record), before they were cut, and were then allowed to regenerate. In a Chase district, the coppice areas were at first for three years totally enclosed, then small 'leaps and creeps' were made, to allow adult deer to leap over or a fawn to creep through; in the final year deer would be allowed free access. When cut, the hazel rods would be sold, until recently at annual auctions, although many farms would get their own thatching spars and hurdles from their own coppices.

In Clapham Wood in Sussex, Mr Juggins, who has made hurdles and then thatching spars there for thirty-five years, still works in his hut in the wood, and has never had a day off for a cold in his life. His stove burns cosily; but youngsters, he says, wouldn't stand the morning frosts – 'They don't want to touch it.' He used to have seven people working under him. His spar hook is probably a hundred years old. His spars go to America,

Coppiced clearing, Clapham Wood

Ireland, France, Germany. He couldn't, he says, live in a city, because of
the noise. The smoke from his hut curls upwards in the coppice, which is
full of sun, spring catkins, peace.

At Sixpenny Handley in Cranborne Chase, Douglas Judd, a hurdle-
maker, still makes thatching spars in the workshop beside his house, the
entrance to which is framed by a curved flint wall. Hazel is now cut all the
year round, he says, instead of from November (after the leaves have
fallen) until March; as a result it now shrinks a little and doesn't last as
long. 'Back in them days, everything got used up'; faggots for cottages,
trimmings for kindling. The mostly self-employed coppice workers in his
district would buy hazel at the annual sale from the Rushmore estate; in
the summer they would work on a farm. Rods for hurdles are first trimmed
and are six feet long and as high as needed. The end rods and those at the
bottom are unsplit; others are split with a spar hook. (Heavier chopping is
done with a nobby hook, and to protect his knees while making spars,

118

Douglas Judd wears a protector made from an old gumboot.) The uprights are driven into holes in a curved billet of wood during the making, so that the whole can stand on this frame; then when the hurdle is flattened out in stacking it will be absolutely taut. It takes just under one hour to make.

When a coppice was left too long before cutting, the hazel was said to have 'got overstood'. Rabbits were at one time a menace; in the last twenty years roe deer have become prolific and eat young shoots. Between the wars 'everything went back – like everything else', and there was a slump in coppicing. Hurdles were in demand for sheep until after the Second World War but now plastic mesh is usually used where sheep are folded. Auctions were suspended after 1970, but the Rushmore estate still has productive hazel which is felled and regenerated in the traditional way. Douglas Judd sends his thatching spars for sale all over the country, and hurdles are in demand for gardens.

In his sweet-smelling workshop with its clean stacks of spars, he will happily talk of his work and of his region. That indefinable fusion of pride in a craft, of country knowledge and humour, fills the silence and floats on the mote-filled air. One looks out of the doorway, and feels momentarily in another and better world, where deer may leap and creep, and men leave wood to grow for the allotted span.

$$6$$

the voices of winds,
trees and birds . . .

William Blake

FLORA AND FAUNA · NATURE RESERVES AND BIRD SANCTUARIES · NATURE
WRITERS

In winter, the voices of wind and trees are loud on the downs. The winds
are biting; walkers reach with relief one of the clumps of beeches, rooted in
a hollow of clay-with-flints, that are now essentially of downland,
although not primevally so.

The wind roars in the leafless branches of the trees like surf. Looking up
is looking upwards into branched seaweed, towards a pale sun. At night,
the clump will be ringed with white shrouds, the fallen leaves underfoot
rimed with frost.

Around, the downs slope bare and forbidding, yet not entirely so. Rooks
and gulls wheel over the last of the stubble, the shoots of new crops. Sheep
graze; heifers nuzzle bales of straw. A solitary rider or runner comes over
the brow of a hill. In a sheltered corner furze is in flower – 'gorse that has
no time not to be gay.'[1] On the high down, lumps of flint lie like bones
chewed by a dog; seared with golden lichen. The grasses of tumuli and
ancient pasture are pale and bent.

Spring, on the downs, the most spectacular of the seasons. In April, the
first cowslips; hairy violets; the small flowers of ground ivy; in dewponds,
water-crowfoot; on woodland scarps, carpets of ivy, celandine, spotted
cuckoo-pint, dog's mercury, moschatel, anemones. Spikes of snowy blackthorn. Birds everywhere, and rabbits in the first sun hardly moving, ears
erect; silhouetted on hind legs against the hawthorn bushes.

In May, the flowering of the wayfaring tree. The electric green of beech
leaves. Campion, in lanes, and lady's smock; beaked parsley, purple bush
vetch, yellow archangels or weasel-snout. The white fire of whitebeams.
Primroses, under the beeches, with wild strawberries, sanicles, violets,
mosses. Woodruff – once used in wine-making, its dried leaves sprinkled
on floors and among linen. On the steep sides of the downs, sheets of blue

Primroses on the
North Downs

121

Germander speedwell; yellow bird's-foot trefoil; clouds of small, hidden, blue or purple milkwort; the first brown skipper butterflies; dustings of sweet vernal grass; false oat grass in sandy pockets; blackbirds and mistle-thrushes in the plough; finches noisy in the hawthorn flowers; skylarks and one swallow; the call of pheasants.

By the end of the month, the first spotted orchis, high on the down or under the scarp; salad burnet; barren strawberries. On roadside verges, or even trunk road cuttings, lady's bedstraw – used in the past for curdling milk, and gathered to fill mattresses – tufted vetch, red clover and lucerne, ox-eye daisies and sainfoin, ribwort plantains. In the woods the pale white helleborine and yellow wood avens. Above newly sown grass, house martins dipping low.

Then all the flowers of summer – the hawkbits and cranesbills, white campion, scabious, marguerites, harebells, ragwort, wild roses; the rare, round-headed rampion, stemless and meadow thistles, clustered bellflowers, fragrant and pyramidal orchids, burnet saxifrage, knapweeds, teasels, self-heal, agrimony, marjoram, thyme, basil thyme; the upright brome, and quaking grass, the common blue butterfly, the rarer blues, the marbled white.

In autumn the last knapweed flowers, the carline thistles, spindle berries, garlands of traveller's joy or old man's beard reaching up to twenty feet high and more between the trees of hangers (its old Dorset name being Devil's guts, or shepherd's delight – the stems used as tobacco). The flocks of migrating birds clustered on wires or flickering over hillsides.

Each region has its own varieties, its own range of species; but over the chalk downlands the patterns and cycles of plant and animal life repeat themselves according to the same rules, and provide the same visual harmony. A fragile harmony; epitomised in the mind's eye perhaps by clouds of sky-blue harebells on their thread-thin stalks, among warm grasses, where small blue butterflies that are growing increasingly rare drift like the essence of summers past – 'the rich blue of the unattainable flower of the sky. . . .'[2]

The pattern is a simple one, based on chalk. Primeval forest cover was cleared on most downs; later trees were also cleared. The deep forested soils eroded, leaving the typical thin calcareous downland soil, which is alkaline. Close nibbling of sheep produces the short turf, and small creeping plants. Taller plants are unable to get established. Grassland on chalk and limestone is especially rich in wild flowers. Some, like the cowslip, disappear when fertilizers are used and the soil becomes too rich for them.

Rabbits were introduced into England by the Normans, and were at first kept in warrens. One finds references such as that to 'the ferme of the

cunnyes' in old documents. Their nibbling, when they later spread over the downs, completed that done by the sheep, until quite recent times when their population decreased. Cattle, on the other hand, pull at grass, making pastures rough, allowing scrub seedlings to remain.

On open downland, ground-nesting birds such as partridge, corn bunting, skylark and meadow pipit breed, and in the valley water-meadows lapwing, snipe, redshank and yellow wagtail. Visiting birds include whinchats and wheatears, and in winter fieldfare and redwing, with geese and duck on flooded areas and in estuaries. Finch flocks congregate over the downs in winter, and the mistle-thrush can be seen there all the year round. In gorse clumps and hawthorn, birds such as linnet, dunnock, yellowhammer and whitethroat are comon, with many other species, as over the arable land, copses and hedges.

An effective food web links downland creatures and plants, since downland is particularly rich in insects – grasshoppers, snails (which need calcium for their shells and are prolific on the downs), ants, bloody-nosed beetles, glow-worms (of which the female gives off a cold light, on warm, still evenings). Rabbits and many insects feed on the plants; birds and shrews feed on the insects; kestrels eat small birds, mice and insects; foxes kill birds, rabbits and small animals. Slugs and snails feed on animal waste and dead plants. The plants seed and are renewed, and spread freely on the chalk, if they are left undisturbed.

It is when this chain is broken, when the old grassland and sheepwalk is disturbed, that wildlife suffers. While downland is so rich in species, it is also particularly vulnerable.

—◇—

'Earth-worms, though in appearance a small and despicable link in the chain of Nature, yet, if lost, would make a lamentable chasm.'　　　　(Gilbert White)

We are not in danger, yet, of losing the earthworm. But we have lost some of our most beautiful or valuable species, and others are in danger of extinction. Cowslips used to be thick enough in many areas to make cowslip balls and cowslip wine in abundance; now to pick a single flower is an offence; on some slopes there may be only one or two clumps. Lapwings, or peewits, with their iridescent greenish-black plumage and white markings – in some districts called green plovers and by the Anglo-Saxons called the *hleapewince* or 'run and wink' – were common on plough until insecticides and machinery drove them off. Now they will nest in meadows and marshes, but where they used to run and twist in great flocks over water-meadows and downland, they are in many places fewer, and the excitement of seeing their speckled eggs on the ground is less frequent.

The stone curlew (or 'thick-knee' as countrymen called it), which loves open flinty downland grass on which to nest, and on which Gilbert White remarked, is reduced to a few pairs scattered along the downs. In Sussex, for example, with the extensive agricultural changes since the war, a population estimated at sixty pairs in 1938 had slumped to twenty to twenty-five pairs by 1964 – with perhaps half that number now, mostly nesting in arable crops.

There was also a sharp decline of birds of prey in the late 1950s and early 1960s, attributed to the use of persistent organo-chlorine seed dressings. The peregrine falcon disappeared as a breeding bird and sparrowhawks and kestrels decreased. (Both have increased in the past decade – kestrels now soar above steep scarps, or even road cuttings.) The sales of the most harmful chemicals were banned or reduced; nationally the peregrine population has recovered to about two thirds of its pre-war level but they have not returned to southern England.

On Salisbury Plain, the rare hobby can be seen near clumps of trees, and the breeding population may have recently increased in Sussex. The hen-harrier is often seen in downland areas in winter. Buzzards, systematically exterminated by gamekeepers in the nineteenth century, have re-established themselves in small numbers to the west.

Swallows have suffered from the loss of sites in traditional barn eaves. Other birds from loss of hedgerows, or diseased elms. Birds that can adapt, or that, like the collared dove, do not mind urbanisation, will survive. For the rest, we will be left with a less varied bird population in a more uniform habitat. A hard winter, such as some recent ones, additionally causes devastation among the smaller birds.

Butterflies, one of our best barometers of healthy or ruined habitats, are in decline. The chequered skipper has been extinct since 1976, and the large blue since 1979. Now the Adonis blue, which likes high temperatures on a sunny slope where sheep have grazed, has been reduced to a very small number indeed (three or four sightings only, in East Sussex, for instance, in 1981), while the common blue, whose caterpillar feeds on bird's-foot trefoil in old pasture (which plant like others disappears when pasture is converted to ley and sprayed with selective herbicides), is less common than it used to be. Twenty-four types of butterfly depend on plants growing in old pasture; none thrives in heavily fertilized rye grass. Moths, too, thrive on old downland. Many have pretty names – Mother Shipton, burnet companion, 'pretty chalk carpet', 'dark brocade'.

When the downland cycle is broken, the bare hills take on a scruffy, undefined look. The insect and bird life suffer; flowers decrease. Modern farming methods tend to destroy habitats, although many farmers are increasingly aware of this and will try to get better yields from existing ground, rather than using every last untreated inch. Arable itself need not be scenically disastrous: sometimes the lines of plough or crops even add to the bold sweep of downs. But arable alone, or arable with leys, can never provide the ecological and visual variety that is downland. More traditional grazing is vital if downland as we know it is not to disappear. The National Trust is one body that with assistance from the Nature Conservancy Council now has grazing flocks on several downs – White Downs, Surrey; Box Hill; Fontmell Down. Local councils are also keen to preserve downland. A 'flying flock' – which could be managed by a shepherd on horseback – has been suggested for the East Sussex downs. (Among other schemes is that of Adur District Council, who with advice from the Sussex Trust for Nature Conservation have begun to clean up Mill Hill in Shoreham, where scrub is encroaching on a valuable habitat.)

It has been estimated that about half of the Wiltshire downs were ploughed between 1937 and 1971, one quarter of Dorset's downs ploughed between 1957 and 1972. In 1980 alone, 32 per cent of Dorset's Sites of Special Scientific Interest were damaged or destroyed. (Since 1811, over 80 per cent of Dorset's heaths.) We have about four thousand SSSIs in Great

Britain; in 1980, the Nature Conservancy Council estimates, about 20,000 acres of land designated in this way was damaged.

The sorry tale of Sladden Wood near Alkham in Kent, has been well documented.[3] Tucked into the North Downs, it contained the rare lady orchid (which can reach to 3 feet in height), with other orchids, green hellebore, nightingales. In 1977, a new owner moved in his bulldozers to fell the trees, even as Dover Council tried to serve a Tree Preservation Order on him (he had, he claimed, mislaid his spectacles). The stumps have been reprieved by High Court injunction. At Graffham Down in West Sussex, a much loved tract of down was cleared despite public protest.

Where landowners can claim compensation for not pursuing schemes harmful to wildlife, the question of finance becomes crucial. It remains to be seen how much or how little the controversial Wildlife and Countryside Act will be able to protect sites. (The Nature Conservancy Council has asked the Government for £20 million to help protect sites over the next decade. To date, grants to the Council have been roughly comparable only to the annual increases given to a body such as the Arts Council.) Many parts of the Act are regarded as a step forward by conservationists, however – for instance, all landowners will now be informed by the NCC of any features of particular ecological value in the land they own.

Downland has suffered from our National Parks system. This covers about 9 per cent of England and Wales, a higher proportion than in other countries. But no downland is included, and the system appears to have been influenced by a founder-member at the planning stage, John Dower, who had a preference for 'wild country' such as Snowdonia and the Lake District. And by America, where, as John Steinbeck pointed out, 'Yellowstone National Park is no more representative of America than is Disneyland'.[4]

In 1947 a government committee recommended that the downs of Sussex and Hampshire should become a national park. The idea was turned down in the 1950s. It is perhaps too late for some areas. But the South Downs in particular, within such easy reach for Londoners, still very much unspoilt over some of their extent, cry out to be made into a national park. This should be done before it is too late. Areas for recreation and mental refreshment may be the most vital ingredient of human lives in the automated centuries ahead, not to mention wildlife.

On the bonus side, examples of many of the unique features of downland have miraculously escaped destruction, have been preserved by one means or another.

At Parham Park, there is probably a survival of one of the rare areas of original pre-Neolithic oak–hazel forest of gentler downland slopes, that

Poppy

There are similar clumps in Wiltshire – 'the rather formal topknots of the Wiltshire summits'.[5] Beech avenues, too, are charismatic on or near downs. In Savernake forest; by Badbury Rings.

Yews, and juniper, are typical downland trees. At Kingley Vale,[6] in a National Nature Reserve on the summit plateau and some slopes of Bow Hill (an outlier of the South Downs), are trees that have been described as the finest natural yew forest in Europe. Kingley Vale was a favourite locality of Sir Arthur Tansley, the first chairman of the Nature Conservancy (now the Nature Conservancy Council); a memorial stone to him stands at the head of the vale. Kingley Vale became in 1952 one of our first nature reserves.[7] Some of the trees in Kingley Bottom may be 500 years old; here the soil is rich and deep, having been washed down from the slopes during the last Ice Age. On the thinner soil of the slopes grow bee orchids and early purple orchis. About forty species of bird breed in the reserve. Deer, foxes, badgers, stoats and weasels are found there. A stoat is sometimes seen in ermine, its pure white winter coat.

A country park that out of season is full of space and solitude, is the Seven Sisters Country Park, where the Cuckmere or 'Snake River' meanders in its perfect ox-bow to the coast. Here poppies and daisies flower on into November. There is chalk pasture, shingle, salt marsh, open downland and cliff. A badger sett and woodland walk. Another good (summer) woodland walk is that at Woods Mill, the headquarters of the Sussex Trust for Nature Conservation, below the South Downs.

Of bird reserves and sanctuaries, one of the most interesting is in the Fleet, the saltwater lagoon 8 miles long between the Chesil Bank and the Dorset coast. Here in the swannery is the only place in England where the social breeding of Mute Swans takes place. Other birds recorded include red-throated diver, wigeon, mallard, whimbrel, red-breasted merganser and goldeneye. At Arundel, the Wildfowl Trust has a reserve where there is a colony of black-necked swans. The RSPB have a reserve at Radipole Lake, Dorset. At Pagham and Chichester harbours the bird life is of international importance, in particular for the dark-bellied brent goose, of which 10 per cent of the world population visits this area in winter.

At Amberley Wild Brooks, in the Arun Valley, the Sussex Trust own some of the land. Here are marsh birds, with in winter wild duck and up to ninety-five of the beautiful Bewick's swans from the Arctic. It is an area flooded in winter and spring, lush with rare plants, the cut channels crossing flat land. In summer it can be baked dry, scorched and brown; but still rich in wildlife such as dragonflies (seventeen species breed in the dykes), and the rare great-crested newt, which it is hoped will survive there. Fifty-six per cent of the entire British aquatic flora grow at Amberley, with sixteen of the species being national rarities. In its setting, with its rushes and grasses, with Amberley Mount and the downs fringing the levels, it is supreme not only for botanists. In 1977 the Southern Water Authority prepared a pump drainage scheme that would have destroyed the wetland wildlife; the outcry from conservation bodies led to a public inquiry, at which the Sussex Trust presented much of the evidence. The scheme was subsequently turned down. (On a smaller scale, a quiet stretch of river bank at Bury, looking across the water to Amberley church and castle, has been preserved and was landscaped by the parish in 1977, safeguarding an area that might have become misused or vandalised.)

While country parks, museums and nature reserves, often referred to as 'honeypot attractions', are one answer to the problem of a large population of people with increasing leisure who want to get out into the countryside, they are still nevertheless one step removed from nature in the wild, or from a solitary enjoyment of that wildness.

The essence of downland is its loneliness, its individuality. And in a civilisation, as H. J. Massingham pointed out, 'whose mechanical forces are hostile to the individual life', 'it is inconceivable that the downs could be enjoyed or convey something of their spirit except for men and women, together or alone, whose mental life is personal and judgment their own.'[8]

For them it is vital that the last untamed areas should not vanish or be increasingly built over, changed. That in river estuaries waders and other birds should not be driven out by power boats and noisy camp sites. That hang-gliders and cars should not take over the high downs.

Some of the greatest pleasures the downs have to offer are not spectacular gatherings of rare species, but the ordinary downland plant or bird met with by chance as an extraordinary bonus in an over-civilised world. Traveller's joy in a downland lane; an unexpected orchid; the countless mosses that grow round the boles of beech trees (that the Victorians had time to list, but ourselves less often; one noted at Wolstonbury in the last century was of a type not growing elsewhere north of the Colosseum in Rome); the dunlin leaving imprints on ice-bound estuary mud; the small golden and flame-crested birds of the gorse – goldfinch, goldcrest, yellowhammer – which pick up the sharp yellow colours of their habitat. The rhythms of the seasons, seen over the whole large downland pattern. The momentous annual events such as the lambing season or the migration of birds when, from Beachy Head for instance, birds set out to cross the Channel to fly to areas such as the South of France or the north coast of Africa. Resting for a few days on the downs, they take advantage of the last

Beech roots with mosses, Wolstonbury Hill

clumps of trees and bushes, where they can feed on insects and berries, before using the uplifts of warm air to rise high in the sky (less high in bad weather) for their flight, which may be at 20, 30 or 40 miles an hour. Cold winter winds sometimes cause havoc among them, and casualties can be found along the coast and over their route (past records note a particularly bad year when dead birds were swept up in their thousands in Rome and other Italian towns). In the spring, they plump down thankfully on outlying land such as Beachy Head or Selsey Bill, and can again rest in the clifftop and downland scrub.

To see swallows and martins congregating at the migrating season, flying so low and so fast over downland slopes that they narrowly miss your head, quartering the air, then perching on wires in rows, is totally absorbing. Or to see the starlings that set out in the morning in flocks to search for food, then retrace their flight in the evening to perch in trees, sometimes so thickly clustered that they resemble a mass of Christmas fruit on the branches, against a lamplit winter sky. The hovering of the windhover or kestrel. The thrush, crushing snail shells and hitting them on its 'thrushes' anvil' or 'slaughter stone' of flint. The call of the cuckoo, forerunner of summer.

'The wild life of today is not ours to dispose of as we please. We have it in trust. We must account for it to those who come after.' King George VI.

Of species which we have lost, some were, or were regarded in the past as, vermin or predators; some were hounded for other reasons. The wolf – always regarded as vermin. The wild boar – no longer one of the royal beasts of the forest. The marten – nearly extinct by the eighteenth century, as 'their skins were too valuable for them to be suffered to exist,' and further decimated by gamekeepers in the nineteenth (but returning now in some wooded areas of the north). Hawks and falcons, which we now know do little harm, used to be shot on sight by gamekeepers of the past. But gamekeepers now are in general good naturalists, killing humanely and with discrimination. The brown rat, fox, grey squirrel and carrion crow are harmful to eggs or young game birds; stoats and weasels are also controlled by gamekeepers. Deer, which are the largest of our remaining wild animals, are carefully managed; deer control societies organised co-operatively by landowners and those with specialist knowledge, en-courage owners to carry out control with experienced stalkers using the permitted high velocity rifles of suitable calibre. Annual censuses are taken and a healthy breeding stock maintained.

Deer in England are basically woodland animals. After roaming free in royal forests and private chases, and later being kept in deer parks, they have in many cases regained their ancient wild status. During the twentieth century it has become difficult to maintain deer parks; deer have broken out, and now roam many of the wooded downs, particularly in areas such as Cranborne Chase, in Hampshire and West Sussex. Around Uppark, for instance, which has not been a deer park for over twenty-five years, wild fallow deer range over a wide area, and in Surrey there is a small wild population of red deer between Haslemere and Farnham, descended from deer which earlier escaped from a park near Godalming.

Red deer, however, don't like the dry downland areas; they are now in general confined to the New Forest and high moors. The favoured breeds on the downs are fallow (with several varieties of colour, in particular the common fallow, which is a dappled fawn in summer, and the black fallow, a smoky grey in winter and even darker in summer), and the roe deer.

Roe deer are intensely shy and wild, and do not run in herds as fallow do. They never thrived in parks, and during the eighteenth century became almost extinct. In 1800 Lord Dorchester released some, starting a new trend in hunting, and others were released in other areas. A number probably escaped from Petworth Park, which is large enough for roe to exist there alongside fallow of several colours. Now they are on the increase in West Sussex, particularly west of Arundel, and along the northern escarpment of the downs. They are colonising westwards across Hampshire, and in Dorset they are once again more numerous than fallow. Coniferous plantations are a good habitat for them, and they don't harm crops as much as fallow deer by lying down in them.

Two other breeds of deer which may run in the wild are muntjac and sika. The muntjac is an Asian species, under 20 inches high at the shoulder, which was introduced at Woburn and has since spread to areas in the south. It travels by night, lying up by day in tall crops or woodland, and keeping to family groups rather than a herd. Sika deer, a little smaller than fallow, were introduced from Japan, and are now found wild in many areas. A gardener in Dorset called us to see sika with their pale fawns, in the moonlight, happily chewing roses. Market-gardeners and farmers will also have ambivalent attitudes to deer. They also damage young trees by browsing, and rub off bark when they are working the velvet from their antlers or making territorial markings. A balance has to be kept.

'Our sport was very good and in a romantic country, for the prospects are noble and vast, the downs stocked with numerous flocks of sheep, the turf rich and fragrant with thyme and burnet ... nor are the nut-brown shepherdesses without their graces. ...' John Aubrey's remarks on natural history are too much coloured by the liveliness and civilised curiosity of his mind to strike the modern reader as particularly scientific or revealing. But they make good reading and, spiced with gossip about people and coloured by his view of the world, they give a keen picture of the natural scene as regarded by men of his century.

'In the gravelly stream at Slaughtenford are excellent troutes; but, though I say it, there are none better in England than at Nawle, which is the source of the streame of Broad Chalke. . . . King Charles I loved a trout above all fresh fish; and when he came to Wilton, as he commonly did every summer, the Earle of Pembroke was wont to send for these trowtes for his majesties eating'.

'We have great plenty of larkes, and very good ones. . . . They take them by alluring them with a dareing-glass. . . .' 'Snails are everywhere; but upon our downes, and so in Dorset, and I believe in Hampshire . . . in the summer time are abundance of very small snailes on the grasse and corne, not much bigger, or no bigger than small pinnes heads. . . .' 'A plaster of honey effectually helpeth a bruise.' 'No snakes or adders at Chalke, and toades very few'. 'Broome keeps sheep from the rott . . . they doe leave a border of broome about their grounds for their sheep to browze on, to keep them sound.'[9]

After his father's death, Aubrey lived at Broade Chalke, but as he had countless friends with whom he stayed, other neighbourhoods come

Fallow deer, Parham Park

vividly into his notes. 'Albury – So called, say some, from the Alders growing about it . . . a most romantick wild Place. . . .' 'Wotton – This Place takes its Name from the vast Quantity of Wood (mostly *Beech*) that surrounds it. . . .'[10] He rarely finished his sentences; his life was too full, as Edward Thomas pointed out, of 'gratitude, hero-worship, curiosity, love-making and litigation'.

With a life in its way as full, but much more serene, Gilbert White, a century later, stands at the threshold of the golden age of natural history writing. His Selborne, bordered as it is by oak forest, heaths, chalk downland, water-meadows, encapsulates the English landscape at its gentlest and best. 'Nothing', wrote one of his earliest admirers, Cobbett, 'can surpass in beauty these dells and hillocks and hangers.' In the garden of Gilbert's house, The Wakes, birds sing joyously in a timeless landscape.

Gilbert White's sundial, The Wakes, Selborne

Gilbert White knew the downs well, having at one time held a curateship at West Dean, near Salisbury, from where he rode to Selborne. He also travelled from Selborne every year to stay with his aunt Mrs Snooke at Ringmer, and his notes on her tortoise Timothy are some of his most delightful. (He once wrote a letter signed Timothy, to a friend's daughter.)

'It does not appear to eat on hot days'; 'May 30th . . . Tortoise eats all day. . . .' On her death, his aunt left him her tortoise, and he watched and cared for him daily, even putting him in a tub of water where he was 'quite out of his element and much dismayed'. Timothy was once missing for a week, but then there is the cryptic note: 'Timothy found.' (Timothy lived longer than White. On the tortoise's death, Timothy was discovered to be female.)

After riding to Ringmer, White makes entries in his journal: 1769: 'Ringmer. Sussex. Sep 18. Bustards on downs. . . . Sept 26. Sweet day. The sheep about Lewes are all without Horns: & have black faces and legs. Sheep have horns and white faces again west of Bramber.'

From about 1770, his sight was deteriorating, but on 13 November 1771, he was still counting sixteen fork-tailed kites together on the downs.

In the affectionate way in which he writes of his parish and its wildlife, as well as in his acute observations, his work is unique. His curiosity about the life and personalities of birds and animals, his way of seeing them as creatures who might have feelings as sensitive as those of men, was new, and has never been surpassed. It hardly matters that he thought swallows did not all migrate: modern scientific knowledge can never equal his 'secret delight' in nature.

He was no recluse. He was pleased in 1788 to note that his nephews and nieces numbered fifty-one. A beautiful girl of 20, who stayed in Selborne in 1763, described a dance at White's house: '. . . danced till 3 in the morning. . . . Never had I such a dance in my life, nor ever shall I have such a one again I believe. . . .' And she describes a walk in the neighbourhood. 'In the evening walked to Noar Hill. Oh sweet evening, sure there never was anything equal to the romantickness of that dear dear hill; never never shall I forget Empshott and the gloomy woods, the distant hills, the South Down.'

Before Gilbert was 12, he had planted an oak and an ash in his father's garden. In later life he sowed beech mast in the hedgerows and bare parts of the downs. In 1793, before he died, his bed was moved into the old parlour at the back of his house, so that his beloved hanger was in sight.

In 1887, Richard Jefferies wrote an introduction to *The Natural History of Selborne*. Born a little over fifty years after Gilbert White had died, his view of the world is very different. No longer the genial, harmonious eighteenth-century view, but a romantic, passionate identifying with a world that was already changing. Perhaps no other writer on the countryside can mean as much to our age, because Jefferies was writing of a way of life, an old agricultural scene that was doomed, and he was writing largely for townspeople for whom nature might be a new experience, a threatened joy.

He was born on Coate Farm in Wiltshire (now a museum) in 1848. His father was a keen observer, eccentric and of a philosophical turn of mind. His mother was town-bred, unhappy on the farm. Richard had no desire to be a farmer, and escaped on long excursions into the countryside – a tall, shambling, meditative youth, whom the locals called the 'Belgian lamp-post' after he had visited the Continent. He never lost this solitariness; but country people colour his writing and he was befriended at Coate by a gamekeeper on the neighbouring Burderop Estate, who formed the inspiration for *The Gamekeeper at Home*. Jefferies made copious notes; became a newspaper reporter at 18; but most of his work was written in recollection. *Bevis* (based on his own boyhood experience of Coate Reservoir) is a brilliant, never-to-be-forgotten book. His writings when he had left Wiltshire for Surrey, and later Sussex, often look back to the Wiltshire scene, the Wiltshire downs he knew so well.

'There the view was over a broad plain, beautiful with wheat, and inclosed by a perfect amphitheatre of green hills. . . .' 'There were grass-grown tumuli on the hills to which of old I used to walk. . . . The sun of the summer morning shone on the dome of sward, and the air came softly up from the wheat below . . . the lark's song like a waterfall in the sky. . . .'[11]

He wrote novels (some unpublished), factual-fiction, autobiography, and over three hundred essays, before his death at 38, as if in a fever to communicate his passion for the countryside and his union with it. He was increasingly ill fom 1881 onwards; some of his last works had to be dictated.

He is not pedantic about nature; sometimes admits to not knowing the name of a flower; is sparing with names of places. In his writings it is possible to experience the actuality of a scene, to be there. His limpid prose goes beyond the visual, formulates the incoherent, pushes back the frontiers of thought. He is the most modern of writers, with a stong streak of prophecy.

From 'To Brighton' – 'There is always hope in the hills.' 'Hope dwells there, somewhere . . . in the breeze, in the sward, or the pale cups of the harebells.' From 'Wild Flowers' – 'Give me the old road, the same flowers . . . there has been a place in the heart waiting for them.' 'Where there are beech trees the land is always beautiful.' And the glorious repetition of the phrases describing the song of the lark: 'the songs of the larks fall as rain', 'There is sunshine in the song; the lark and the light are one'; 'pours forth a rain of unwearied notes. . . .' And 'Nothing despairs but man'. 'Seldom do we realize that the world is practically no thicker to us than the print of our

Early morning, South Downs

footsteps on the path. Upon that surface we walk and act our comedy of life, and what is beneath is nothing to us. But it is out from that underworld, from the dead and the unknown, from the cold moist ground, that these green blades have sprung.' 'The wind passes, and it bends – let the wind too, pass over the spirit.' [12]

Jefferies would have us all live a life with time to stand and stare. He was aware of the encroachments of the mechanised world, the pitfalls of human attitudes. 'An endless succession of labour . . . shall we never know how to lighten it, how to live with the flowers. . . .' ('The Life of the Fields'); 'The greatest obstacle to progress is the lack now beginning to be felt all over the world, but more especially in the countries most highly civilized, of a true ideal to work up to' ('Nature and Eternity'). 'We may then look to a time when farming will become a commercial speculation, and will be carried on by large joint-stock concerns. . . .' ('The Future of Farming'). 'It is the lie of a morality founded on money only. . . . Many superstitions have been got rid of in these days; time it is that this, the last and worst, were

Wild thyme

eradicated. . .'; 'The moment the eye of the mind is filled with the beauty of things natural an equal freedom and width of view come to it. Step out upon the broad down beside the green corn and let its freshness become part of life.'[13]

W. H. Hudson, who much admired Jefferies (and was buried, in 1922, in the same cemetery, at Broadwater), wrote that 'Even the "lardy cakes" from a village baker's seemed finer food because Jefferies had known them and deplored their increasing rarity.'[14] (They can still be found in several counties.)

Hudson's own work is less etherealised than that of Jefferies. More analytical. He does not give us the beautiful litany of the sound of the lark, but more precise description – 'The song of the lark is a continuous torrent of contrasted guttural and clear shrill sounds and trills. . . . The acutest note of all, a clear piercing sound like a cry several times repeated, is like a chance patch of the most brilliant colour occurring at intervals in the pattern . . . subtle, insistent, filling the world and the soul, yet always at a vast distance. . . .' (A sound that has obsessed many, including the American John Burroughs, who came to England wishing to hear the song of the nightingale, but could not find one, except in the zoo. The lark he heard: 'One of my best days in England was spent amid the singing of skylarks on the South Down Hills . . . the song disappointed me at first . . . a little stubbly . . .' then 'a perfect swarm of notes pouring out like bees from a hive . . . our birds all stop when the skylark has only just begun . . . almost as unceasing as the light of a star.'[15])

Born in South America, Hudson observed England with the freshness of a traveller – each scene in his prose books a brilliant tone painting of an animal, bird, insect, or human being. He loved the space of the downs; the 'wild ancient charm of Salisbury plain'; the stories he heard of people of 'better, less civilized days'. In *A Shepherd's Life* he wrote:

> The final effect of this wide green space with signs of human life and labour in it, and sight of animals – sheep and cattle – at various distances, is that we are not aliens here, intruders or invaders on the earth, living in it but apart, perhaps hating and spoiling it, but with the other animals are children of Nature, like them living and seeking our subsistence under her sky, familiar with her sun and wind and rain.

He was an early supporter of the RSPB. He had been invited to 'Fur, Fin and Feather afternoons' by a group who plied him with 'daintily served' meals in return for inspiration. The Society for the Protection of Birds was founded in 1889 (by women pledged not to wear feathers of birds not killed for food – excepting ostrich) and in 1891 the Fur, Fin and Feather group joined them. Hudson, a member of the Council, raised the society's standing, wrote for them, and left them £6000 in his will. Unlike Jefferies, who had been taught to shoot vermin, Hudson abhorred shooting, often made efforts to have a pet bird released from its cage. He wrote, 'Sussex has distinguished itself above all counties . . . in the large number of native species it has succeeded in extirpating during the present century'. And in *Hampshire Days*, where are some of his most acute descriptions of insects and birds, he perhaps for the first time in a book states clearly and categorically that birds can suffer as much as humans. 'It is not only that this inconceivable amount of bird life must be destroyed each year, but we cannot suppose that death is not a painful process . . . in that mysterious green world we, too, live in and do not understand, in which life and death and pleasure and pain are interwoven light and shade.'

On the downs, the mysteries of 'The blue sky, the brown soil beneath, the grass, the trees, the animals, the wind, and rain, and sun, and stars', were 'never strange' to him. There he could enjoy the cirl nestling, of black and crimson, the young snipe 'in down of brown-gold, frosted with silvery white', the turtle-dove, the glow-worm 'shining with a strange glory', the flock after flock of migrating swallows 'shooting past my head with amazing velocity'; the 'immemorial fascination' of the chalk hills.

7

Work will go on here with God-speed . . .

William Blake

ARTISTS WRITERS MUSICIANS · THE INSPIRATION OF THE DOWNS

To the artist, writer, musician, the downs have offered the same qualities, sometimes to a heightened extent, that they offer to everyone who knows them. Escape and revelation.

Generations of creative minds have found peace and space among the calm green hills that 'glimmer in a summer gloaming'. Some, like Oscar Wilde ('I hope to do work there. The house, I hear, is very small, and I have no writing room. However, anything is better than London.')[1], or even Blake, have chafed at the lack of city vitality, even while drawing on those inspirational springs which well forth only in solitude. '. . . you, the gilt and graceful boy, would be bored,' Wilde told 'Bosie' (Lord Alfred Douglas) in a letter from Worthing, where he was writing *The Importance of Being Earnest*, which, he told another correspondent, 'as it is quite nonsensical and has no serious interest, will I hope bring me in a lot of red gold'.[2] And to another, 'I can't come up to town, I have no money.'[3]

A landscape of renewal. People have painted the downs, have written about them; have, living among them, written of entirely different things. But those artists who have experienced to a deeper degree the intangible spirit of the downs, have been changed, whether they liked it or not; have undergone a spiritual metamorphosis that has marked their work with something aerial and, if they were great artists, immortal.

> *Rarely, rarely, comest thou,*
> *Spirit of Delight!*

—◇—

'When the golden mists are born. . .'

William Blake went down to Felpham, in Sussex, in 1800, when he was 43, for three and a half years – his only time out of London. He had been introduced to the poet and essayist William Hayley, who had moved to Felpham from his estate at Eartham under the South Downs, and for whose life of Cowper Blake undertook to do illustrations.

Blake stayed in a small thatched cottage, and to the Londoner born and bred, this new life, close to the hills which he surely visited with Hayley, was transforming.

'Felpham is a sweet place for Study, because it is more Spiritual than London. Heaven opens here on all sides her golden Gates. . . . And now Begins a New life, because another covering of Earth is shaken off.'[4] 'We travel'd thro' a most beautiful country on a most glorious day. Our cottage is more beautiful than I thought it . . . the sweet air & the voices of winds, trees and birds, & the odours of the happy ground, makes it a dwelling for immortals. Work will go on here with God speed.'[5]

He was working on miniatures, engravings, watercolours, and it was during this time that his two last prophetic books, *Milton* and *Jerusalem*

'The happy ground. . .'
Rackham Hill

(which he thought his best) began to be formulated. His mystical dreams were heightened here, and the shadows of men appeared to him in the countryside around him. On one of the pages of *Milton* he drew his cottage, with a naked image of himself walking in the garden, and the image of an angel about to alight in a tree.

Down-like hills can be seen in illustrations such as those to Hayley's *Little Tom the Sailor*; and in 'Landscape near Felpham' (1800). An engraving for another ballad shows Chichester Cathedral. A needlework piece after a design by Blake is of downland hares. And in all his work after this time in the country the trees and hills are more lifelike: the stifflly etched trees of his earlier work have become the wild, curving arms of downland beeches. The woodblocks to *The Pastorals of Virgil* show sheep, hills, trees, a winding river, a church spire, oxen, thatched cottages – 'O lovely Felpham, to thee I am eternally indebted. . . .'

An unfortunate libel action marred the end of Blake's stay. But he had been marked more deeply than by external things. He wrote many poems, and was filled with a great outburst of prophetic inspiration. He had seen a world 'With happiness stretch'd across the hills. . . .'

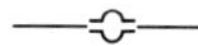

'I am in solitude and poverty, but very fat and well . . . I feel more energetic and ambitious for excellence in art than ever . . .' '. . . the green mountains that glimmer in a summer gloaming . . . seem the interchangeable twilight of that peaceful country, where there is no sorrow and no night.'[6]

Among the North Downs, not the South, the painter Samuel Palmer found happiness. But there is a particular type of countryside, a particular hour of day in the hills, that is Palmer, which you find in several downland regions. The hour when the sun is setting; gilding the shoulders of the downs; above them the moon rises in the twilit sky; the haze of thickets and trees becomes black; a rabbit emerges; sheep close in for the night; a single figure in the fields. A treed landscape, of the smaller, perfectly formed downs. Compton Down in West Sussex, for instance, which seen at the season when beeches become copper beacons, with the inky scrub running up its smooth dome, a moon rising in a warm sky, imprints itself indelibly on your mind. A herd of white cattle grazing in the fields nearby assures you that this is an etching of the dream world which the old painters saw.

A valleyed landscape. Samuel Palmer found his 'Valley of Vision' at Shoreham in Kent, between the North Downs. Before the coming of the railways, quite cut off, surrounded by cornfields, among wooded slopes. '. . . the rising moon with raving-mad splendour of orange twilight-glow on the landscape. I saw that at Shoreham,' he wrote. The seven years he spent there were the happiest of his life, and the years of his most brilliant achievement.

He lived with his father, at first in a small thatched cottage, spending eight shillings a week each, their food being mainly eggs, milk and fruit. With the friends who came down to visit him, he went for long night walks in the hills. Palmer grew a beard, and hair to his shoulders, and amazed the villagers, who would hear him singing at dawn as he returned from a night in the open air.

'Tho' living in the country, I really did not think there were those splendours in the visible creation which I have lately seen', he wrote in 1829.[7] He sketched outdoors, then painted his landscapes at home – works such as 'The Harvest Moon', 'The Bright Cloud', 'A Landscape Twilight', 'The Flock and the Star', 'The Shearers'.

In later years, in a rapidly suburbanised Redhill, Palmer lived and painted with 'the memory of a vision'. When villas were built outside one of his windows, when he was over 70, he had the glass whitewashed. He would walk into the country, and in old age in his garden, and liked then to be driven into the neighbouring downs, where the beeches and yews reminded him of the Kentish Shoreham. 'More and more', said his son, 'he nestled in the past', and he noted that on the day when his father was buried at Reigate, 'It was a warm showery May morning . . . and high in the sky above the green turf and the elm trees, a lark was singing.'[8]

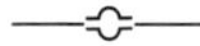

Palmer had moved to Shoreham because of bronchial trouble. A later painter who sought 'peace and a bit of silence', at intervals during his London life, was Burne-Jones, who with his wife Georgiana stayed at North End House at Rottingdean often between 1880 and 1898. He was visited there by William Morris, Rossetti, Millais and Ford Madox Brown. (A later writer at North End House was Enid Bagnold, whose *National Velvet* is the story of a girl in a downland village such as Rottingdean. Young Velvets still, of course, fiercely range the Sussex hills.)

Burne-Jones said of the view from his window: 'Opposite the window is a holy Church and at the back of it a holy Down, both most bonny to look at – and so I look almost all the time.' He disliked the turmoil of Brighton, and crowds. 'I hate and loathe winter and everything about it – its beef, its balls, its parties, its mincepies . . . its Bank holidays, its home holidays, its rain, wind, cold, sleet . . . mud, charities, clerical opportunities . . . but . . . rooks look happy. . . . Two black oxen drawing a cart have just passed. . . . I don't want much in this world – I like black oxen drawing carts.'[9]

But summer he liked: 'It was all like one day, nothing happened, the sun beat upon the hills, and they were covered with wheat-sheaves, making tears gather to the eyes. I had my Book of Flowers with me and designed five new ones –'[10]

His flower book was, his wife wrote, perhaps 'a fuller expression of himself than exists elsewhere in his work'. He devised watercolour designs to represent the folk names of flowers – many of the scenes being downland landscapes, in which cloud shapes, grasses and wind, move over the page. 'Ladder of Heaven' – a soul climbs a rainbow in a downland scene studded with plants. 'Morning Glories' – angels spread out the clouds at dawn over bronzed hills. 'With the Wind' – Dante's vision of Paolo and Francesca, an intermingling of shapes and shadows, grasses and figures. And 'Golden Greeting', or 'Meeting after Death'. 'I wish Golden Greeting were quite true – just as I did it I wish it might really be. Nothing else will ever be what I want but that.' (One can excuse Georgiana's note of satisfaction, 'we all recognized the portrait', concerning his painting, a watercolour head, of 'The Spirit of the Downs'.)

Evening scarp, from Newtimber Hill

—⚬—

What is this spirit? At its most basic it is perhaps a sense of euphoria, a clarity, that comes from walking on the hills. Hills which are easily accessible, and when reached, visually stimulating in a way which never cloys. When walking on the downs, in their heady air, you feel that you could walk to the edges of the earth and beyond.

'Oh! the Downs high to the cool sky!' wrote Galsworthy in his well-known poem. 'And the feel of the sun-warmed moss. . . . And the beech grove, and a wood-dove, And the trail where the shepherds pass. . . .'

Some poets of the downs have cultivated a companionable marching rhythm redolent of the pipe and jar at the inns where they might call in. One can see them marching over the hills with their rucksacks, a book of poetry in one pocket, notes for an article in a literary magazine in the other. Verse not entirely fashionable today. At its best, very fine. Belloc's 'Ha'nacker Mill':

> *Sally is gone that was so kindly*
> *Sally is gone from Ha'nacker Hill.*
> *And the Briar grows ever since then so blindly*
> *And ever since then the clapper is still . . .*
>
> *. . .*
>
> *Spirits that call and no one answers;*
> *Ha'nacker's down and England's done.*
> *Wind and Thistle for pipe and dancers*
> *And never a ploughman under the Sun.*
> *Never a ploughman. Never a one.*[11]

(Halnaker Mill is now repaired. The ploughmen, enclosed in their tractors, live on.)

Hilaire Belloc's love for his 'own country' is very moving:

> *and of mine opulence I leave*
> *To every Sussex girl and boy*
> *My lot in universal joy.*
>
> *. . .*
>
> *One with our random fields we grow.*
>
> *. . .*
>
> *He does not die that can bequeath*
> *Some influence to the land he knows,*
> *Or dares, persistent, interwreath*
> *Love permanent with the wild hedgerows.*[12]

At its most ethereal, most intangible, the spirit of the downs is something other-worldly, ancient, free. Critics and biographers have gone to lengths to explain that our most aerial poet, Shelley, was born in Sussex, but did not write *about* Sussex, either the wooded country around Field Place, near Warnham, where he was born, or the downs within sight of the estate. Yet how could the boy who lived in the district until he was 10, who later roamed the woods and hills on moonlit nights during his – somewhat melancholy – school holidays, not absorb the particular quality of nature to be found there? It is not coincidence that some of his finest poetry immortalises the west wind, the skylark, the moon; that he was one of the first writers to reject 'observations' for a modern feeling of affinity with nature; that his images, when he was far away in Italy, follow a stamp that must have been impressed on his subconscious years before: '. . . we love the flowers, the grass, the waters and the sky. In the motion of the very leaves of spring, in the blue air, there is then found a secret correspondence with our heart. . . .'[13]

The boy who told other children stories about the Tortoise of Warnham Pond, or the Great Old Snake of Warnham Wood, whose love of paper boats persisted into adulthood so that he once floated a five-pound note on the Serpentine; who read his book while he should have been learning to shoot (the gamekeeper obligingly gave the day's bag as 'fallen to Master Bysshe'); who wrote to a friend in 1809, 'I have an excellent subject for a poem, & in these "woods & wilds and solitary groves" will apply to the Muse...'; who mistook a girl seen wandering on the downs for a ghost – became the man who personifies the 'eloquence of the tongueless wind', the free spirit of the landscape of the mind's eye.

> *I love all that thou lovest,*
> *Spirit of Delight!*
> *The fresh Earth in new leaves dressed,*
> *And the starry night;*
> *Autumn evening, and the morn*
> *When the golden mists are born.*[14]

In our own day, the poet Ted Walker also spent a boyhood within sight of the South Downs, seen from the south, from Lancing and Shoreham. They were, he says, 'what I could see when I was growing up, in the distance – a kind of far-off country.' At 14 he walked in a straight line north to the top of Lancing Ring and on past Steep Down, sleeping out – 'I suddenly became aware of this place where I belonged, that I had never seen.' In his autobiography, *The High Path*, he eloquently describes not a fulsome English landscape, but the man-made, timeless landscape where his roots lie.

> On the Downs, when I was alone, I escaped not only from the ordinary daily slots I moved through but also, it seemed, from time itself. I entered a world and an era not my own and yet disturbingly familiar. The Downs are numinous hills. Even today, for all the

fell-booted ramblers traipsing from Harting Hill to Beachy Head, they contain an immense solitude; you can walk for hours through the strange combes and hangers or even along the exposed and well-trodden Ridgeway without being impinged upon by another living soul. Yet you move among multitudes; and whether or not you believe in ghosts as such, you would have to be spiritually dead not to have a sense of the men of prehistory who lived and worked here . . . when I followed the upward tracks, I did not have to search so minutely for the traces of much more ancient men. The desolate paths which led me to Cissbury had once led warriors to the flint mines for their weapons. Elsewhere I clambered linchets, circled hill-forts, lay upon the barrows – burial mounds of the neolithic princes – listening to the clamour of their silence.[15]

'. . . that violent shock of the beautiful but inhuman which we have when suddenly the tall hare leaps across our path, or the dog fox's bark on the Downs makes twenty centuries of civilization nothing' – wrote Edward Thomas. A shock felt by many writers – who, in the past, seemed to go enthusiastically out of their way to meet it. It was not only Mad Shelley who walked by moonlight. The Wordsworths, Coleridge, diarists; their pages full of moonlit rambles and homecomings by starlight.

Dorothy Wordsworth, that intrepid walker by moonlight, perceived with this sense of fresh awareness the landscape round Pilsdon Pen in Dorset, where she lived with her brother William from 1795 to 1797, at Racedown Lodge, going there when she was 23. 'I think Racedown is the place dearest to my recollections upon the whole surface of the island: it is the first home I had.'[16] 'We walk about two hours every morning. . . . We have hills which, seen from a distance almost take the character of mountains, some cultivated nearly to their summits, others in their wild state covered with furze and broom. These delight me the most. . . .'[17] She was 'riding sometimes, hunting, coursing, cleaving wood', besides being occupied with her domestic cares. Her journals were not started until she moved to Alfoxden, near Nether Stowey, but her writing then and ever afterwards was a continuation of this sharp awareness that she found at Racedown. 'Walked upon the hill-tops; followed the sheep tracks till we overlooked the larger coombe . . . locks of wool still spangled with the dewdrops . . . the sheep glittering in the sunshine.'[18]

William meanwhile, whose spiritual home was to be the grander scenery of the Lake District, wrote at Racedown: 'We plant cabbages . . . you may perhaps suspect that into cabbages we shall be transformed.'[19]

Different minds, different scenery. Some, without Dorothy Wordsworth's practical streak, have been led by the downs to purple flights of fancy. Charlotte Smith, the poetess who lived much of her life near Chichester and in Brighton, having married at 16 a West India merchant who was subsequently ruined, supported her family with aplomb. Her 'Sonnets' were an instant success when published in 1785. 'Ah! hills beloved! – your turf, your flowers remain' is one of the less romantic lines of her poetry.

Then Hayley, a vogue in his own day. William Collins, of Chichester. Swinburne, whose 'Seamew' of Beachy Head takes one aloft, even on its nineteenth-century wings – 'Ah, well were I for ever, Wouldst thou change lives with me'; Francis Thompson; 'The hills look over on the South, And southwards dreams the sea. . . . Oh, there were flowers in Storrington/On the turf and on the spray'; George Meredith, who lived at Flint Cottage, Box Hill: 'I am in deep woods / Between the two twilights' (his *Diana of the Crossways* has a North Downs setting).

More recently, Andrew Young (*A Prospect of Flowers*), and John Betjeman, who has sung of Dorset villages – 'Down the grass between the beeches, mellow in the evening hush'.[20]

Yeats found inspiration at Steyning, in 1938, when he stayed at Chantrey House. 'I have a one-act play in my head, a scene of tragic intensity, but I doubt if I will begin it until I get to Steyning. . . . My recent work has greater strangeness and I think greater intensity than anything I have done.'[21] In 1819, Keats had found inspiration at Chichester, where he stayed at two different houses. 'Nothing worth speaking of happened at either place – I took down some of the thin paper and wrote on it a little poem call'd "St Agnes Eve".'[22]

> *The hare limp'd trembling through the frozen grass,*
> *And silent was the flock in woolly fold. . . .*

That year, and earlier, he was also at Shanklin on the Isle of Wight, which he thought 'a most beautiful place', and where a strip of grass was named after him, Keats Green. He wrote to Fanny Brawne: 'I am now at a very pleasant cottage window, looking on to a beautiful hilly country, with a glimpse of the sea. . . .' These Isle of Wight downs were also promoted by Tennyson, that great strider in hat and cloak. At Farringford House, Freshwater (a place George Morland the painter had discovered half a century before and from which he had explored every last corner of the island), much of Tennyson's work was written. He wrote to a friend in 1854, inviting him to stay – 'Where, far from smoke and noise of town,/ I watch the twilight falling brown/ All round a careless ordered garden, / Close to the ridge of a noble down.' And in Sussex, his verse sang of the view from Blackdown over the Weald: 'You came, and looked and loved the view /Long known and loved by me. . .'

His walking habit, and that of other creative minds, is a link with many writers of the past, who roamed afield for inspiration. The travellers – Lambarde in Kent, Aubrey, Celia Fiennes, Defoe, Ruskin. And the poets, from Sir Philip Sidney, with his 'table book' in which he wrote while out hunting on Salisbury Plain, onwards. William Barnes, the Dorset dialect poet, walked about his parish near Dorchester well into his eighties, dressed in caped cloak, breeches, buckled shoes, and with a leather satchel. He claimed he was proof against all weathers. 'I knew you young, and love you now, O shining grass, and shady bough.'

The renewal, exhilaration, offered by the downs. Found by Romney, many of whose paintings are at Petworth, when he stayed at Eartham, in the 'fine balsamic air of Sussex'. By Constable, who noted that Brighton was 'a wonderful place for setting people up. . . . Old Neptune gets all the ladies with child'. By Robert Louis Stevenson, who often stayed at the Burford Bridge Hotel at the foot of Box Hill. By T. E. Lawrence, whose retreat at Clouds Hill in Dorset was within reach of the hills.

Turner, at Petworth, found an inspiration which led to a change of style, the development of his later work. In his small interior scenes, outlines are blurred, brilliant whites set off the warmer colours. His study for the 'Old Chain Pier, Brighton' (Tate Gallery), has great delicacy and luminosity, a luminosity which increasingly filled his work, and which he perhaps found to perfection in the soft misty light to the seaward side of the South Downs. Ruskin has left a charming account of Turner at Petworth. After fishing in the park at sunset, 'Turner became quite chatty, rigging me a little ship . . . making her sails from a leaf or two torn from a small sketch-book.' They then trooped back to the house, Turner carrying a pike in one hand, a roll of sketches falling from a pocket in his coat tails, which he then tied up with fishing line.[23]

Also important to painters, the vegetation of the downs – the windswept trees, gnarled roots, grasses, herbs, moonlit copses. A mysterious, dense yet magical quality conveyed in many of the works of Arthur Rackham, who spent much time in the early years of this century at an old farmhouse at Houghton, in Sussex; and by Reynolds Stone, among whose works are illustrations to *A Shepherd's Life*. Paul Nash painted striking and symbolic scenes of the Wiltshire, and other, downs, and Eric Ravilious (once his pupil) semi-abstracts of the chalk-hills, as for example the powerful 'The Vale of the White Horse' (1939; Tate Gallery).

Musicians, too, have responded to the sight, to the presence of the downs. Edward Elgar moved to Brinkwells, near Pulborough, in 1917. From there he could see the South Downs – 'I have never seen anything so wonderful as the sun climbing over our view in golden mist.' He relished his life there. 'I make huge fires in the wood, meanly delighting in the fact that I can burn more than anyone I know.' There he wrote his great Cello Concerto, in 1919, his last major work. Nostalgic, mellow, glorious, its intertwining themes rise like smoke from his bonfire, soaring and sad, with the rumblings of war, and notes fading like the mist on the downs, the last

Arcadia – Wilton

sparks and embers of the 'days that are gone'. The days to which the Great War had put an end. For all the popularity of his music, Elgar never evaded complexities, suffering, the un-banal. He wrote of a rehearsal at Wembley Stadium in 1924: 'The King insists on Land of Hope, and there were some ludicrous suggestions. ... But everything seems so hopelessly and irredeemably *vulgar* ... hammering, loud speakers, amplifiers, four aeroplanes circling over – all mechanical and horrible. No soul, no romance, and no imagination.'[24]

Those he could find elsewhere. As did John Ireland, who lived at Washington, a little farther along the same range of downs. (It was there he wrote his Downland Symphony.)

The euphoria, the poetry of the downs, has been matched for many artists by an earth-bound reality. Thomas Hardy, born in the 'long low cottage with a hipped roof of thatch', its doorway 'worn and scratched by much passing in and out, giving it by day the appearance of a keyhole'[25] – the cottage at Higher Bockhampton which, surrounded by old apple trees and rustic profusion is still an idyll – was well aware, not only of the harsher side of rural life, but also of its grim tragedies. Much of his prose work had origins in the stories told him by his mother about life in her youth, and her mother's youth, while his paternal grandmother, Mary Head, who is likely to have been part of the inspiration for his heroine Tess, had not only had an illegitimate child but had been committed by magistrates on the charge of stealing a copper kettle, which if she had been convicted could have led to her death by hanging. (A woman in the same year was sentenced to death for stealing a silver button.) In the varied lives of his many Dorset cousins; in the realities of his own experience – when a boy in the 1840s, for instance, Hardy knew a shepherd boy who died of starvation; in tales of a previous generation (his father had been present in his youth at the hanging of four men who had merely been present when others set fire to a rick); through newspaper cuttings and through his own knowledge of the new industries in a town such as Dorchester, Hardy could find dramatic instances of the only too real fates of people who lived in his Wessex, whether in town or country. But his father, a master mason, introduced him to the Dorset hills which became a loved territory to him, symbolic of that side of his genius which he expressed most profoundly in his poetry.

His father would carry a telescope, and the young Thomas could study those sweeping views which he later defined for all time – the 'great and particular glory' of his Egdon Heath – the dark blue shadowy expanse, which seen from the chalk downs to seaward, by Lord's Barrow perhaps, is still today (except, sadly, for Winfrith Heath Nuclear Research Station), one of the inspiring views of southern England. Fold on fold of tree, mist and low heath, to 'the distant rims of the world and of the firmament'.[26]

As a boy, Hardy was close to the natural world – rabbits, glow-worms, adders, newts. He was desolated to see a dead fieldfare in icy winter; once in the fields on his way to Puddletown, he knelt to eat grass among the sheep, to try their world, much to the sheep's astonishment. (In later life he and his first wife had a succession of cats; his second marriage was blessed with 'Wessex', a terrier which had a fixed habit of biting people.) Hardy was a keen bicyclist into his eighties, an enthusiasm shared by his first wife Emma, who even took her green bicycle to the Continent.

Nature, for Hardy, is always closely linked to human destiny. In times of hardship, Tess is among the wintry Dorset uplands, when 'Every twig was covered with a white nap as of fur'. In earlier days of fulfilment, she is in the lush valley of the Frome, 'a level landscape compounded of old landscapes long forgotten', rampant with milk and buttercups – a landscape for which one feels Hardy secretly longed, among his dreams of fair

Thomas Hardy's Cottage, Higher Bockhampton

153

women. Spiritual fulfilment came for his heroine at Stonehenge, at dawn on the great plain, as it came to Hardy on the Wessex heights, the symbol of and for his poetry.

—◇—

'Strange how the savage England lingers in patches:' wrote D. H. Lawrence in the title story of *England My England*, 'as here, amid these shaggy gorse commons, and marshy, snake-infested places near the foot of the south downs. The spirit of place lingering on primeval, as when the Saxons came, so long ago.'[27]

The story is set at Greatham: a young couple, Egbert and Winifred, live in an old Hampshire cottage 'that crouched near the earth amid flowers' and amid 'flamy vegetation'. A place of fierce seclusion and savage peace, where Egbert feels the desire for 'old gods, old, lost passions . . . all the lost, intense sensations of the primeval people of the place.' Later, he dies in Flanders, in a setting reminiscent of the shaggy gorse at home. 'The gorse bushes on either hand were dark, but a few sparks of flowers showed yellow. He noticed them almost unconsciously as he waited, in the lull.'

The places of the mind's eye. Places on or near downland made memorable for ever for us by writers such as Kipling, R. D. Blackmore (*Alice Lorraine* and Chanctonbury), Harrison Ainsworth (*Ovingdean Grange*), George Moore (*Esther Waters* and Buckingham House, Shoreham), Rosemary Sutcliff (*Knight's Fee*: Arundel and the Adur Valley). It was at the Elms, Rottingdean, that Kipling wrote, among other works, *Kim*, and many of his poems. He had spent summer holidays as a boy with his aunt Georgiana Burne-Jones, and in turn sent his children for 'jam-smeared picnics' on the downs. His 'blunt, bow-headed, whale-backed Downs'.

—◇—

'Each day is . . . full of wandering clouds; and that fading and rising of the light which so enraptures me in the downs; which I am always comparing to the light beneath an alabaster bowl'. 'I walked to the racecourse today and saw a weasel'. Walking, bicycling, living 'lapped in peace' at Rodmell, in the wide valley of the Sussex Ouse, where she found reprieve from stress, and from the busy-ness of London, Virginia Woolf saw the fluid shape of her great novel *The Waves*, in which reality flashes as brilliantly as sea water, or the river glinting in its marshes.

> Often down here I have entered into a sanctuary . . . of great agony once; and always some terror; so afraid one is of loneliness; of seeing to the bottom of the vessel. That is one of the experiences I have had here . . . a thing I see before me . . . beside which nothing matters; in which I shall rest and continue to exist. . . . And I fancy sometimes this is the most necessary thing to me: that which I seek.[28]

'The city of a dream. . .' Gold Hill, Shaftesbury

Many Bloomsbury friends visited her and Leonard Woolf at Rodmell, as they did her sister Vanessa Bell at Charleston, also near Lewes. Monk's House, Rodmell (now owned by the National Trust), was a cold place at which to stay. One unlucky visitor, trying vainly to warm himself at the 'Cosy Stove' in his bedroom, burnt his trousers.

At Steep in Hampshire, within sight of Butser and neighbouring downs, lived Edward Thomas, who perhaps more than any writer has given us the essence of the hills of the south – by introducing and commenting on other writers such as Gilbert White, Jefferies and Hudson, and by his own poetry and prose. Meditative, austere and reserved (yet his books are peopled by encounters with men, women and children), he was most himself when alone in the country. In her moving introduction to *The South Country* by her husband, Helen Thomas writes that '*The South Country* is one of the happiest of the prose works of Edward Thomas . . . and was, as not many of his books could be, written for his own pleasure'. Before Steep, he had lived for five years in Kent. He was killed at Arras in 1917, aged 39. Having left home 'to go to France, farther south, but not to *his* south; the compass is not the index of the heart.'[29]

'. . . almost his greatest pleasure, and certainly his greatest need,' Helen Thomas continued, 'was to walk and be alone in the country he has called "The South Country" ['all that country which is dominated by the Downs, or by the English Channel, or by both'].'

He wrote of the downs: 'most admirably themselves when they are bare of all but grass and a few bushes of gorse and juniper and some yew, and their ridges make flowing but infinitely variable clear lines against the sky.'

Of the lark: 'Often when the lark is high he seems to be singing in some keyless chamber of the brain. . . .'

Of Hampshire: 'The pale stubble is yellow and tenderly lit, and gives the low hills a hollow light appearance as if they might presently dissolve.' 'larks building spires above spires in the sky. . . .' 'Catch at the dreams as they hover in the warm thick air . . . two columns of blue smoke from two white cottages among trees. . . . The dreams are over them. . . .'

And of Kent: 'Then the North Downs come in sight. . . . They are suffused in late sunshine, their trees misty and massed, under a happy sky. . . . The mind takes flight and hovers among the leaves.'

On the Pilgrim's Way: 'In the east the sun rises, a red-faced drover and a million sheep going before him silent over the blue downs of the dawn.'

Of Surrey: 'Then I saw a huge silence of meadows, of woods, and beyond these, of hills that raised two breasts of empurpled turf into the sky'; 'I like to think how easily Nature will absorb London as she absorbed the mastodon, setting her spiders to spin the winding-sheet and her worms to fill in the graves, and her grass to cover it pitifully up, adding flowers. . . . I like to see the preliminaries of this toil where Nature tries her hand at mossing the factory roof, rusting the deserted railway metals. . . .'

And in Sussex, having left London in a train, where 'The railway carriage was nearly full of men reading the same newspaper under three or four different names', '. . . The dust from the high road powders the nettles and perfects the arresting melancholy of the desolation. . . . But above are the Downs, green and sweet. . . . The highest points command much of earth, all of heaven'; 'an old woman sits on the grass, her feet in the dust at the edge of the road . . . she sits by the wayside eternally, expecting nothing'; 'blackbirds that have a wilder song in this world of infinite corn below and grass above'; 'something in me belongs to these things'.[30]   *Amberley Wild Brooks*

Helen Thomas thought of him when 'standing at the entrance of his dugout, he looked north and saw, or dreamed he saw, Sussex, with her gentle downs . . . and Kent . . . Hampshire with her hangers of beech and yew . . . and Wiltshire . . . these dear places he was never to visit again.'

Now all roads lead to France
And heavy is the tread
Of the living; but the dead
Returning lightly dance:

Whatever the road bring
To me or take from me,
They keep me company
With their pattering,

Crowding the solitude
Of the loops over the downs,
Hushing the roar of towns
And their brief multitude.[31]

8

Scatter my ashes!

John Galsworthy

GRAVES AND BURIALS · DEATH SPIRITS GHOSTS · FERTILITY AND REBIRTH

'Let them be free to the air . . .' Galsworthy's poem seems very close to the thinking of late-twentieth-century man; it is certainly close to the eternal spirit of the downs.

A pantheistic longing to be united with the world outside nudges our thoughts, our beliefs. Space travel may prove elusive for a few more generations, even undesirable, but at least in death we might travel beyond an earth-bound grave (if, that is, we face up to death at all); we might, then, perhaps be close to the most serene, yet most haunting and haunted landscapes we know.

An individual death must have reached its apotheosis in Victorian – if not Elizabethan days. The gilded, emblazoned tombs of Elizabethan swashbucklers and merchants appear a mite less enclosed than the heavy slabs protected by railings in which eminent Victorians lie, their spouse beside them, the world shut out. A complete antithesis to the ashes flung to the cool winds, the small casket aligned with others (to which we are returning), the communal feeling of an individuality which may have been burdensome to carry, mingling with others to make way for rebirth, new lives, new growth. Will we go farther still towards great communal ceremonies, to appease the fates, to celebrate the coming of the sun, to consecrate our hallowed places?

The world has greater memorials to the dead than West Kennet, and more celebrated ones, but very, very few of such massive simplicity and dignity – or age. . . . The little cells inside the barrow have long been bereft of their bones by the archaeologists, yet death still lingers in their air – but it is not death the horror, the dread marauding skeleton on horseback. Here one feels a very long, quiet peace, almost a domesticity, a sleeping stone womb.[1]

Richard Jefferies's grave, Broadwater

The West Kennet Long Barrow, one and a half miles south of Avebury –
a stone-chambered tomb for collective burial, of about 2500 BC. The finest
megalithic tomb in England and Wales, housing many burials over several
centuries. Very long, crowning a low hill; in the distance its portal stones,
in sunlight, as regal as stones at Mycenae. Softly covered with meadow
cranesbill and knapweeds.

Before the megalithic tombs (megaliths being huge stone blocks), were
the earthen long barrows. Bodies were often stored in mortuary enclosures
or stockades of wood, until the flesh disintegrated. The bones were then
placed in a wood or turf hut, under a covering mound of chalk or earth.
Long barrows are found on the downs in Sussex (Bevis's Thumb; on
Windover Hill; on Firle Beacon, for instance), in Kent (Jullieberrie's Grave),
and all over Wessex – on the Hampshire Uplands, Salisbury Plain, the
Marlborough Downs and in Dorset. In Dorset the long barrows were
sometimes especially long, known as bank barrows. Barrows were set on
the brow of a hill, dominating the surrounding land, and would originally
have been of shining white chalk. They are still impressive, as on
Thickthorn Down in Dorset.

The defleshing of the corpses was in order to free the spirits of the dead.
From under the earth came the seeds of new growth, of the spring, which
would be protected by these spirits. Their tombs were cult centres for the
living, as well as graves, and offerings might be made at the blackest time
of the year, the midwinter solstice, to ensure the return of the sun. Possibly
even human sacrifices were made, since the skulls of many skeletons show
evidence of heavy blows.

The megalithic tombs were more sophisticated structures, perhaps only
for tribal leaders. They could become tribal vaults for future generations, a
marker for the family's land. In the south-east, Kit's Coty House is an
important, if imperfect remains of a megalithic burial chamber. The
Coldrum chamber tomb near Trottiscliffe is another.

Round barrows were introduced in Late Neolithic times. The Beaker Folk
buried their dead singly under round barrows, with pottery of the beaker
type, sometimes golden ornaments. The great chieftains of the Bronze Age
used several types of round barrows; males were buried in bell-barrows (a
vertical cross section would give the outline of a bell); women in disc
barrows with a small central hump, or saucer barrows. One of the finest
cemeteries is on Oakley Down in Dorset, in that curious area near the
meeting place of the Roman Ackling Dyke and the Dorset Cursus, one of
those long ways edged with ditch and bank, whose purpose is unknown to
us – possibly they were Neolithic processional ways, or for funeral rites.
The Dorset one is the longest in Europe. On near-by Wyke Down are
several more barrows, and throughout the Wessex region are good
examples – the Five Marys which stand outlined on a ridge to the north of
Chaldon Herring; near Stonehenge, and Avebury; on Snail Down on

Ramparts at Maiden Castle

Salisbury Plain (partly destroyed by tanks), and elsewhere on the plain; near Lambourn (the Lambourn Seven Barrows), and along the Ridgeway. In Sussex, the Devil's Jumps at Treyford Hill are one of the main groups in southern England. In Surrey, round barrows have been found at sites such as Wotton, Banstead, Frensham. Some are damaged: at Puttenham (Frowsbarrow), the bowl-barrow has been in turn desecrated by a stone commemorating Queen Victoria's visit in 1857, and by a golf-tee.

Few traces of Early and Middle Iron Age burials remain. Ashes may have been scattered, or bodies exposed in shrines to disintegrate. The Belgae of the Late Iron Age cremated their dead and enclosed the ashes in pear-shaped pedestal urns. Their priests were the Druids, for so long mistakenly associated with the building of Stonehenge. In the burial vaults of great leaders were placed food and wine, bowls and jugs, jewellery, clothing and musical instruments. The Belgic tribes were among the first to introduce gold, silver and bronze coins, and from those bearing the names of their leaders, we have the first names in English history.

—◇—

163

Of the ceremonies that accompanied burial, or commemorated it, we know little. As Aubrey Burl evocatively puts it, 'it is like trying to touch shadows to see in the dark the people who have gone and who left no word or sound behind them.'[2] William Stukeley, the antiquarian, who first saw Avebury in 1719, made meticulous plans, but became so obsessed with his idea that the Druids had built the stone circles that he later falsified measurements. His 'final diorama', says Burl, '. . . looks more like an alert octopus than the megalithic complex it really was'. (The same author also disagrees with the 'ley-line' theory.)

But the truth is likely to be stranger. If the Wicker Image, first sketched in 1676 (in Aylett Sammes's *Britannia Antiqua Illustrata*), showing bodies caged to be burnt in a 'wicker man', is mythical, human sacrifices can't be ruled out, since the curled skeletons of strangers (representing the corn spirit) have been found buried beside standing stones, as if to placate the

Stonehenge

gods. By making comparisons with primitive societies in other parts of the world, archaeologists can conjecture that witch-doctors or medicine men carrying axes aloft and with antlers on their heads may have led firelit processions during which they performed initiation rites with domestic animals and humans. Dancers may have circled round the holy places, and between the stones of avenues, the stones themselves being in alternating male and female shapes. Certainly sexual initiation and fertility was associated with death. Chalk phalli and figurines have been found in pits, with other offerings such as antlers, rich soil, fruits, broken twigs. And the ceremonies, which must have changed from culture to culture, were, from what we can tell from later myth and superstition, associated with the great seasonal climaxes – the harvest of the autumn, the cold and sterility of midwinter and the regeneration of spring. Rituals to appease nature, since to prehistoric man the real and the supernatural intermingled. The later Celts had four great nature festivals, in February, May, August and the end of October, and in Celtic myth handed down by word of mouth, gods and heroes lived in the earth or in tombs. Beliefs about death and fertility lingered on until medieval times and later. Holed stones, ring stones, horn-dancers, earth goddesses, legends. And the early Christians were so aware of this that they often built churches inside or on top of Neolithic or other monuments. (As at Knowlton in Dorset, where a ruined medieval church stands inside a banked circle, probably a henge monument, surrounded by wide cornfields, a tree-clad tumulus, summer poppies. A fertile place still, in this most fertile county.)

The great primeval symbols of death and rebirth, of day and night, were inevitably the sun and moon. Were the great centres such as Avebury and Stonehenge observatories? Vast calculating centres of prehistoric peoples?

Avebury is the largest British stone circle. Of the two avenues of stones originally running from it, one led to a stone circle Sanctuary (no longer standing), the other to the Longstones west of Beckhampton. A temple for nearly a thousand years, an absence of weapons and finds of domestic pottery confirm its ceremonial use. From the great circular ditch, the builders had removed enough chalk to build a pyramid, and the original ditch would have been deeper than the height of a house.

Stonehenge is the most important prehistoric monument in Britain. It was built in five successive stages, over about seventeen centuries between about 2800 and 1100 BC. (First a bank and ditch, the Heel Stone and the so-called Aubrey Holes, with probably a ceremonial gateway. Then the building of two circles of bluestones, with an entrance, pointing towards the rising sun at midsummer. Thirdly, a lintelled circle and horseshoe of large sarsen stones, on the same midsummer sunrise axis, followed by a further rearrangement of bluestones, which had been dismantled. Then the final reconstruction, with an inner horseshoe of bluestones within the sarsens, and also a bluestone circle.) The bluestones were ferried, possibly over a long period, from the Prescelly mountains in Wales. The sarsen stones have been squared and dressed with heavy stone hammers, in a way unknown then outside the Mediterranean area. (One of the carvings on the sarsens is of a dagger of a kind found in the shaft graves of Mycenae in Greece.) The lintels are held on their uprights by mortice-and-tenon joints worked in the stone, and are locked end-to-end by tongue-and-groove joints. The pillars taper upwards, increasing their apparent height.

There is no conclusive evidence of astronomical purpose at either site, especially at Avebury. The historian Diodorus, in the first century BC, referred to a famous temple of Apollo (Stonehenge?), where the moon was also worshipped – 'the god visits the island every nineteen years'. A primitive calculator perhaps, which with alignments to the midsummer sunrise and midwinter sunrise, would enable men to foretell the seasons in those ages when the changing cycles were so vital to crops and to life, and when perhaps men dreaded yearly that the sun would not come back.

Even if there was no such sophisticated purpose, it seems natural that the people who used these great monuments would incorporate the sun and moon, the stars and eclipses into their design, perhaps unconsciously, perhaps as artists, as anyone who had seen the rising or dying sun striking between the tapering stone trees of Stonehenge would know. Possibly it is good that, in a world which distrusts answers, Stonehenge remains, in John Fowles's words, 'a blank sheet of paper – in a world where, in terms of knowledge, blank sheets become increasingly rare things.'[3]

'The old White Horse wants setting to rights, And the Squire has promised good cheer, So we'll give him a scrape, to keep him in shape, And he'll last for many a year.'[4]

The other enigmas of the downs.

Silbury Hill – cleverly constructed from cells filled with chalk rubble – 35,000,000 basket-loads of it, taking an estimated 18,000,000 man-hours to build. John Aubrey recounted 'the tradition only is, that King Sil or Zel, as the countrey folke pronounce, was buried here on horseback', from which grew a legend that a golden horseman was to be found at the mound's centre. But no burial has been found, in several excavations.

The Cerne Abbas Giant, whose full frontal outline is splendidly displayed across 180 feet of a Dorset hillside. Victorians let the grass grow over his private parts, and in one book he was depicted as if wearing swimming trunks. Today he is again shameless. (Some have thought he represents a Celtic version of the Graeco-Phoenician king-demigod Heracles, but there is reason to suppose that the figure was cut at the end of the second century, when the Emperor Commodus fancied himself as Hercules. May-day ceremonies have been traditionally associated with the 'Trendle', an Iron Age burial ground above the figure.)

More modest, although Kipling described him looking 'naked towards the shires', is the Long Man of Wilmington in Sussex. Restored in 1874, the figure may be Romano-British, or may once have held spears and represented the pagan god Woden. Sussex was the last of the kingdoms to relinquish pagan beliefs.

And the horses of the downs. Westbury, Cherhill, Hackpen, Osmington, Marlborough, among them, all of different dates. Echoed in our century by regimental badges cut in the chalk – leaving what message to posterity?

Most mysterious, elusive of all, the White Horse of Uffington. Very early, of no later than the Late Iron Age. Stylised, bird-headed, flying, it would seem to have been created to be seen from the sky.

How was it laid out? (It is 365 feet long.) What does it mean? Its disjointed shape is like that of horses shown on coins of the Atrabates, an ancient British tribe. But the legends are legion. St George is said to have slain the dragon on Dragon Hill below the horse. Wayland the Smith of the Neolithic long barrow Wayland's Smithy, one and a half miles away, is said to have made the White Horse's shoes, and if a traveller left a groat on

The Uffington White Horse

167

the capstone of the smithy he could hope to find his horse mysteriously reshod. In his *Icknield Way*, itself a most haunting book, Edward Thomas evokes in his passages on Uffington, the legend of the 'Lady of the Night', who rides followed by her pack of hounds, her black hair streaming behind her, on her white horse.

H. J. Massingham associated the White Horse with a corn-and-fertility goddess of the Celts, descended from the Black Demeter of Hellas. Demeter was a divine mare in primitive myth, and to the Neolithic people of Britain, the goddess of the sky and earth and under the earth had been the guardian of the spirits of the dead. Was the horse carved out for her to see?

Festivals used to be held at the scouring of the horse, every seven years, with horse and ass races, wrestling, and rolling of cheeses down the hill into the valley called the Manger. 'That was a great day, the scouring,' we were told by someone from as far afield as Ramsbury, who used to attend it. The event in 1857 is described by Thomas Hughes in *The Scouring of the White Horse*. (Now it is the task of the Department of the Environment; I have to add that all these hill figures, which need regular weeding and cleaning, are currently far from white.)

---

little, lost, Down churches praise
The Lord who made the hills.[5]

They stand in their peaceful fields, with remnants of beauty and a sunny, well-used air, from the comparatively short period of a few centuries between the dying out of the old pagan faiths and the depletion of their villages. They had their day, and have it still – hammocked among their hills, swifts flying past the small caps or towers, rooks cawing from the surrounding belfries of trees.

The churches were built as the old beliefs lessened their hold. For some of the original races lingered on, and the descendants of the small, narrow-headed Neolithic people led a fugitive existence, becoming the fairies of folk-lore and legend. Cultures merged; Roman urn-fields, as the Saxons finally defeated the last of the Romano-British under leaders such as Arthur, gave way to Saxon burials. These were often on high ground, particularly of great leaders, as at Highdown Hill in Sussex. In Dorset there are fewer traces of early Saxon burial; the county was conquered by the Saxons far later than the other chalk lands of Wessex, the great defensive earthwork of Bokerley Dyke which stretched from Cranborne Chase to the edge of the Dorset heathlands, blocking the main route into the county.

The first Saxon churches have so often been replaced, but details remain. Towers; a flying angel carved in stone, at Winterbourne Steepleton near Dorchester; chancel arches; the nave and porch at Bishopstone near

Newhaven, with over the porch, a sundial inscribed 'Eadric'; sculptured stone at Codford St Peter in Wiltshire. Details of Norman work are scattered more profusely, and from later ages downland churches offer memorable features. Twelfth-century wall-paintings at Coombes in Sussex, close by the nineteenth-century Gothicry of Lancing chapel; a chantry chapel at Boxgrove Priory, with Renaissance-inspired carvings, some, as of boys raiding a pear tree, modelled on old French Books of Hours, and in the same church, twining botanical paintings on the vaulted roof of the nave – daisies, grapes, honeysuckle, roses; eighteenth-century fittings in the Norman church at Winterborne Tomson, Dorset; New Shoreham's fine tower; gargoyles at Cerne Abbas; Burne-Jones's stained glass at Rottingdean.

On a grander scale, the churches of the Wessex 'minster' towns – Beaminster, Sturminster Newton; the abbey churches – Sherborne (once

169

the capital of Wessex), Wimborne; those of the county towns – Lewes, Dorchester; and the cathedrals – Salisbury, Chichester – which seen from the downs form a counterpoint, an ethereal lodestone.

Everyone will have a favourite church, knowing the architecture or mood which means most to him. No one could fail to warm to the most isolated, the least pretentious churches and churchyards, their graves overgrown with long grasses and wild flowers, an aura of homeliness and holiness mingling to give something unique in our noisy life.

Folkington, with its small bell-cote steeple, below the slopes of the South Downs; Friston, with its pond that is protected as an ancient monument – the first pond to be so designated, in 1973; Lullington, now the smallest church in England, a few yards square in a ring of trees, being the chancel of a once larger church; Southease with its round tower, and churchyard awash with snowdrops in spring; Edburton, with interesting scratch dials, and tree-shaded churchyard; in Dorset, Gussage St Andrew, tucked away in a field behind a farmhouse, without spire or tower, and Winterborne Tomson, greatly loved by Thomas Hardy, built on the simplest plan of all, a single cell, with rounded end, small bell-cote, calves chewing in the adjoining barn, and outside, a single large grave – that of Albert Reginald Powys, architect and writer, who saved the church from ruin and was for twenty-five years 'devoted servant' of the Society for the Protection of Ancient Buildings.

'. . . I think I should be tempted to go to church myself if I saw all my neighbours starting off across the fields or along paths that led to such charmed spots,' wrote the American John Burroughs.[6] (Having previously referred to a 'race that knows how to use its feet, and holds foot-paths sacred'.)

If ghosts haunt such churchyards, they are friendly ones.

Despite the erosions of time, relics, superstition and myth have lingered on. Legend tells that when the church at Alfriston was being built, and foundations were dug, all traces of the work were miraculously moved each night to the mound where the church now stands, once a pagan burial site. The legend of the Devil's Dyke is more attractive than the geological explanation for the coomb. The Devil, it is said, cut it to let the

Churchyard – Edburton, Sussex

sea run into the Weald to drown the churches. An old woman, disturbed by the noise, looked out, holding a candle in a sieve. Thinking this was the sunrise, the Devil gave up.

In isolated areas of the downland counties, such as Cranborne Chase, you can see rings of adults and children dancing on Midsummer's Day, and at Ashmore, at 700 feet the highest village in Dorset, built round its pond which has probably been there since Roman times and before, there is danced, on the nearest Friday to 21 June, a Filly Loo, and a green man is built with branches of green leaves.

At Chanctonbury Ring, a hoard of Anglo-Saxon coins was found, where a white-bearded Saxon ghost was said to wander. Skeletons supposedly dance round an oak on the downs on Midsummer Eve.

Philip Gosse and his wife put such legends to the test. 'Naturally the Ring is haunted. Even on bright summer days there is an uncanny sense of some unseen presence, which seems to follow you about . . . on a dark night. My wife and I went there alone. We never shall repeat the visit. Some things are best forgotten if they can be, and certainly not set down in a book.'[7]

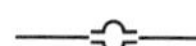

A downland setting has been chosen by generations of people of different temperaments, in which to end their days.

Small graves, ornate graves. A gravestone high on the downs to Wee Tibby and Wee Tiny (who, what were they?). In the church of St John the Baptist, in Kemp Town, a marble memorial of the kneeling Maria Fitzherbert, put up in 1837 by 'One to whom she was more than a parent. . .', her adopted daughter Minnie Seymour. Pale crossed alabaster hands in Worthing; the Gage ram in marble in the church of St Peter at Firle. Near Patcham, under the ridge, close to the sky, the marble Chattri, a dome supported by eight pillars, to the memory of the Indian soldiers who died during the First World War in hospital in Brighton.

One who was not buried in downland, but in Rome, near his friend Shelley, was Edward John Trelawny. He had come to Sompting twelve years before his death, having been sent some figs from there by Rossetti, which he so much appreciated that he bought the garden in which they grew (and the house). Trelawny's life was so colourful that doubt has now been cast on the tales he told of his youth at sea – fighting for a pirate and marrying a 14-year-old Arab girl, Zela, who died when still young. Yet his true later adventures are no less strange – among them fighting for the Greeks with Byron, and marrying the sister of a Greek bandit.

Trelawny admired Shelley above all, and it was he who plucked Shelley's heart from the funeral pyre; he would later show the scar on his hand. In Sompting he painted the ceiling of one room blue as the Italian sky, with trees and flowers on the walls. In the garden he planted a cypress

from a cone from one of the trees he had himself planted over Shelley's grave. He made the garden a bird sanctuary, and in his eighties still swam and walked. More than once he gave away his overcoat to a tramp, and once his new boots, walking home barefoot.

'I am almost constantly in the country on the South Coast within sight of the sea – so you see I am constant to my first love . . . the mind does not age with the body, all my early convictions and feeling harden with my bones.'[8]

For Galsworthy, who was disappointed, not by lack of fame, but by his failure perhaps to be the kind of writer he most wanted to be, and saddened by the years of the First World War, his last home at Bury House in Sussex offered something of what he sought. Seeing the house in its downland setting he said, 'This is the place.'[9] On the downs he could be,

The Gage ram, St Peter's, Firle

173

as he so loved, 'high to the cool sky' and close to 'the lark's song, and the wind song, And the scent of the parching grass!'

Walking his horse beneath the dappled, flickering light of the beechwood, he would become so much at one with beast and tree, and air and sun and shadow, moving, as it were, in a world remote, that a mood of ecstasy, very nearly approaching religious exaltation, would come over his face. And so, reluctantly, with few words, over the clean, smooth, lark-infested edge of the Down, which hung above the marvellous view of Amberley Wildbrooks which he so loved. . . .[10]

Wessex Heights

There he rides free to the air. While in the cemetery at Broadwater, along different paths, the graves of Richard Jefferies and W. H. Hudson lie among rose-garlanded yews, within sight of the downs.

For Jefferies, who died so young, after years of illness, life was not a looking back, although he remembered the old times so vividly, but always a searching, and what he found he has given us. In his most moving essay, 'My Old Village', which it is hard to read without tears, he reveals some of the bitterness of suffering, much of the loneliness of his youth ('there was not a single one friendly to me'), and all of his understanding.

> The ghosts die as we grow older, they die and their places are taken by real ghosts. . . .
>
> . . . I think I have heard that the oaks are down. They may be standing or down, it matters nothing to me; the leaves I last saw upon them are gone for evermore, nor shall I ever see them come there again ruddy in spring. I would not see them again even if I could; they could never look again as they used to do. There are too many memories there. . . . The perch used to drift down the stream. . . . The sun shone there for a very long time, and the water rippled and sang, and it always seemed to me that I could feel the rippling and the singing and the sparkling back through the centuries. . . . There used to be clouds over the fields, white clouds in blue summer skies. I have lived a good deal on clouds. . . . I see clouds now sometimes when the iron grip of hell permits for a minute or two; they are very different clouds, and speak differently. I long for some of the old clouds that had no memories. . .
>
> . . . I planted myself everywhere under the trees in the fields and footpaths, by day and by night. . . . And perhaps in course of time I shall find out also, when I pass away physically, that as a matter of fact there never was any earth.

The essay was published in the year he died. Although he never went back to Coate, he found in the South Downs the images of the downland he had known as a young man, and it was in Sussex that he looked back to write his spiritual autobiography, *The Story of My Heart*, in which he reached out beyond the limitations of the mind in prose so powerful that it carries the most cynical with it.

'Two thousand years! Summer after summer the blue butterflies had visited the mound, the thyme had flowered, the wind sighed in the grass. . . . It is eternity now. I am in the midst of it.'[11]

> Shall I be gone long?
> *For ever and a day.*
> To whom there belong?
> *Ask the stone to say,*
> *Ask my song.*

In the churchyard of St Michael's, Stinsford, in the country of Hardy whom he admired, is the grave of Cecil Day Lewis, Poet Laureate, with this moving inscription.

Within sight of the land he loved, in this same churchyard, is buried the heart of Thomas Hardy, in the grave of his first wife Emma, not far from the cottage where he was born.

> *There are some heights in Wessex, shaped as if by a kindly hand*
> *For thinking, dreaming, dying on, and at crises when I stand,*
> *Say, on Ingpen Beacon eastward, or on Wylls-Neck westwardly,*
> *I seem where I was before my birth, and after death may be.*[12]

There is a spirit of reconciliation on the downs. There, it is easier to see the elusive patterns of existence, the continuity of something for which life is an inadequate word. As the wind blows, as the clouds move, as the eye

176

takes in the great surges of landscape and the star-strewn, flower-studded detail of the turf, it matters less that we will not be here to see future generations of trees, of men walking the old paths, but only that they should still be there. And even these things become symbols for an otherness, a wholeness. All time becomes momentarily immediate; young men stop in their tracks, and old men forget. The sun takes over.

'Haste not, be at rest, this Now is eternity.'
. . .
'It is eternity now. I am in the midst of it. It is about me in the sunshine. . . .'

Photographer's Note

The photographs for this book were taken either with a rollfilm Rolleicord
Vb twin-lens reflex camera (often used at eye-level with a pentaprism) or
with a 35 mm Pentax Spotmatic II using lenses from 28 mm to 300 mm
(one or two in pre-set mounts), some with a 1.5 × teleconverter attached.
Sometimes, where extreme portability was needed, I used a Rollei B35.
Skylight (1A) or orange filters were also used on occasion.

Film for both formats was FP4 developed in Microphen at 1:1 dilution,
or, where necessary, TRI-X (or in some cases Verichrome Pan) developed
in the same developer (35 mm TRI-X in neat Microdol-X).

Quite often I used a large tripod, with legs independently capable of
extension, at any angle in the vertical plane, to achieve a camera height
from ground level up to 9 feet, and adjustable to give a stable position on
uneven terrain and in inaccessible places. A monopod was also very useful
at times, particularly to help keep the camera steady on such surfaces and
when using one of the longer lenses in a brisk wind.

I found invaluable, on the downs, the nearly 6-feet-long thumbstick made
for me (to replace for this work a smaller one I have had for many years) by
Laurie Skeats, the Dorset flockmaster mentioned in the text – invaluable
not only when walking on, that is, up and down, the downs, but also for
propping up or holding down any unwanted but intrusive tree branches,
twigs or vegetation – also for use instead of the monopod with a 200 or
300 mm lens resting in its horn-topped 'V'.

I carried an adaptable folding knife for any 'gardening' necessary before
taking a close-up of plants, etc., the relevant Ordnance Survey 1:50000 or
1:25000 scale maps, a pair of ultra-light binoculars, and a small compass.

To give as firm a foothold as possible on particularly steep slopes, and on
the exposed chalk of the downs which, in certain conditions, is notoriously
slippery, I found 'commando-soled' waterproof shoes or boots very
helpful.

A close companion who can be persuaded to act as a 'human lens shade'
in open country is also very useful!

Necessary attributes for this type of photography are, I feel, the ability to select and to set up the right camera, lens and filter very quickly after, perhaps, a 4- or 5-mile walk; the judgment to choose, following a careful reading of the map, the best route to a certain place, and the best angle for a shot; the stoicism to carry on after reaching it and finding it photographically disappointing; and the opportunism to depart, mentally and physically, from the chosen line to take some different, more stimulating or more interesting shots. Not least, as more than one farmer has rightly stressed to me, the ability to avoid irritating a cow with a young calf or calves. . . .

These photographs are a personal view of the downland of southern England – an area I see as particularly illustrative of the soft English countryside with all its tonal gradations of light and shade – an area of English landscape at its finest.

J.M.

Notes

(Full bibliographical details are given only for those books not included in the Bibliography.)

Chapter 1

1 John Galsworthy, 'Buttercup Night', in *Tatterdemalion* (Heinemann, London, 1920).
2 From Edward Thomas, 'Wind and Mist', in *Collected Poems* (Faber, London, 1974).
3 W. G. Hoskins, *English Landscapes* (BBC, London, 1973).
4 Edward Thomas, *The South Country*.
5 John Aubrey, *The Natural History of Wiltshire*.
6 William Shakespeare, *Henry VI*, Pt. 3.
7 John Fowles and Barry Brukoff, *The Enigma of Stonehenge* © 1980 by the Philpot Museum.
8 Gilbert White, *The Natural History of Selborne*, Letters to Daines Barrington, XVII.
9 John Burroughs, *Winter Sunshine*.
10 Richard Jefferies, 'On the Downs', in *The Hills and the Vale*, 1909.
11 W. H. Hudson, *Nature in Downland* (Dent, London, 1923).
12 H. J. Massingham, *English Downland*.
13 Thomas Hardy, *Tess of the d'Urbervilles* (Macmillan, London, 1953).
14 Written between about 1665 and 1697. MS in Bodleian Library, Oxford. Published with facsimile of MS, Hutchinson and Dorset Publishing Co., 1982.
15 See Aubrey Burl, *Prehistoric Avebury*.
16 Byron, *Don Juan*, XI, 25.
17 Richard Jefferies, 'Out of Doors in February', *The Open Air* (1885).
18 Account of Barclay Phillips, quoted in J. A. Erredge, *History of Brighthelmston*. See also Eliot Curwen and Eliot Cecil Curwen, 'The Hove Tumulus' in *Brighton and Hove Archaeologist*, 1924.
19 See Aubrey Burl, op. cit.
20 See Marion Shoard, *The Theft of the Countryside*.
21 Richard Jefferies, 'Wild Flowers', *The Open Air* (1885).
22 See Mrs Henry Cust, *Gentlemen Errant* (London, 1909).
23 W. D. Robson-Scott, *German Travellers in England* (Blackwell, Oxford, 1953).
24 Nikolai Karamzin, *Letters from a Russian Traveller* (1790).
25 Johann Wilhelm von Archenholz, *England und Italien* (1787).
26 Ralph Waldo Emerson, *English Traits* (1856).
27 Johanna Schopenhauer, *Reise durch England und Schottland* (Stuttgart, 1803).
28 Richard Jefferies, 'Wild flowers'. [The Dyke is the Devil's Dyke, Sussex.]
29 Richard Jefferies, *The Story of My Heart* (Longmans Green, London, 1883).

Chapter 2

1 'Cliffs Rocks Deeps Shallows . . . Sun Moon and Stars and all those sort of things' – Letter from John Keats to Jane and Mariane Reynolds, from Littlehampton, Sussex, *The Letters of John Keats* (London, 1895).

180

2   William Shakespeare, *King Lear*, Act IV, Sc. 6.
3   Tennyson, Sussex from Blackdown, from 'Prologue to General Hamley'.
4   N. Kazantzakis, *England* (Cassirer, 1965).
5   Swinburne, 'On the South Coast'.
6   Ted Walker, from 'Estuary', in *Fox on a Barn Door* (Cape, London, 1965).
7   See Walter Shepherd, *Flint*.
8   There is a fine collection of fossils in Dorchester Museum.
9   From 'The Ruin', in *The Battle of Maldon and Other Old English Poems*, translated by Kevin Crossley-Holland (Macmillan, London, 1965).
10 Freya Stark, *Traveller's Prelude: An Autobiography* (Murray, London, 1950).
11 W. H. Hudson, 'Vale of the Wylye', in *A Shepherd's Life* (1910).
12 William Cobbett, *Rural Rides*.
13 W. H. Hudson, op. cit.
14 Ibid.
15 A. G. Bradley, *Rivers and Streams of England* (Adam & Charles Black, London, 1909).
16 Ibid.
17 Ibid.
18 Matthew Arnold, 'Dover Beach'.
19 Camden.
20 The Rev. William Clark, letter to a friend, 1736.
21 Dr John Burton's Greek diary. Quoted in David Harrison, *Along the South Downs*.
22 *The Diary and Letters of Madame d'Arblay*, with notes by W. C. Ward (London, 1890).
23 Osbert Sitwell and Margaret Barton, *Brighton*.
24 Ibid.
25 *Récits d'une Tante: Mémoires de la Comtesse de Boigne* (Paris, 1907).
26 *Punch*, 1845.
27 William Thackeray, *The Newcomes* (London, 1854).
28 From an aquatint of 1825.
29 Thomas Hardy, *The Trumpet-Major* (Macmillan, London, 1974).
30 Letter to early friends and his wife, 29 August 1823. *John Constable's Correspondence*, edited and annotated by R. B. Beckett, Suffolk Records' Society, 1962–8, in John Lloyd Fraser, *John Constable*.
31 Letter to the Fishers, 28 November 1826. Ibid.
32 Undated letter to the Fishers. Ibid.
33 Letter to C. R. Leslie RA, 16 July 1834. Ibid.
34 Hilary Spurling, *Ivy When Young: the Early Life of I. Compton-Burnett* (Gollancz, London, 1974).
35 Richard Jefferies, 'Sunny Brighton', *Longmans Magazine*, 1884.
36 Richard Jefferies, 'In Brighton', Uncollected Essays.
37 Letter to Louie Burrows, 1910. Both letters quoted in *The Letters of D. H. Lawrence*, edited by James T. Boulton (Cambridge University Press, 1979).
38 Virginia Woolf, *A Writer's Diary* (Hogarth Press, London, 1953).
39 Introductory poem, 'The Downs, The Weald and the Marshes', from *Sea and Sussex – From Rudyard Kipling's Verse* (Macmillan, London, 1926).

Chapter 3

1   Richard Jefferies, 'One of the New Voters', *The Open Air* (1885).
2   William Cobbett, *Rural Rides*.
3   E. Cecil Curwen, *The Archaeology of Sussex* (Methuen, London, 1954).
4   Hilaire Belloc.
5   See Aubrey Burl, op. cit.
6   William Cobbett, op. cit.
7   W. H. Hudson, 'Vale of the Wylye', in *A Shepherd's Life*.
8   Holinshed's *Chronicle*.
9   John Aubrey, *The Natural History of Wiltshire*.

10 Letter to Louise de Kéroualle, n.d. Goodwood MS 3. West Sussex Record Office, Chichester.
11 *Five Hundred Points of Good Husbandry* by Tusser, quoted in Augustus Hare, *Sussex* (Allen, London, 1894).
12 Richard Jefferies, 'Wild Flowers'.
13 John Aubrey, op. cit.
14 John Toland, *The Description of Epsom; with the Humours and Politicks of the Place: In a Letter to Eudoxa* (London, 1711).
15 Mark Girouard, *Life in the English Country House*.
16 Matthew Arnold, 'Thyrsis', *Macmillan's Magazine*, 1866.

Chapter 4

1 W. B. Yeats, Paul Rutledge in 'Where There is Nothing', *Collected Plays* (Macmillan, London, 1934).
2 . Edward Thomas, *The Icknield Way* (Constable, London, 1916).
3 Ibid.
4 Edward Thomas, *The South Country*.
5 Hilaire Belloc, *The Old Road*.
6 Edward Thomas, *The Icknield Way*.
7 Ibid.
8 See Christopher Taylor, *Roads and Tracks of Britain*.
9 From 'The Historical Account of the Rise and Progress of the Charlton Congress', quoted in David Hunn, *Goodwood*.
10 Fuller, *The Worthies of England* (London, 1662).
11 Adam Badeau, *Aristocracy in England* (New York, 1886).
12 *Goodwood: Royal Letters*, edited by Timothy J. McCann (1977). Goodwood MS 819.
13 H. Taine, *Notes sur l'Angleterre* (1862).
14 Johann Wilhelm von Archenholz, op. cit.
15 See John Marshall, *Sussex Cricket*.
16 *Sussex County Cricket Club Hove 1872–1972* (SCCC, Hove, 1972).

Chapter 5

1 W. H. Hudson, 'The Living Garment', in *Nature in Downland* (Dent, London, 1923).
2 W. B. Yeats, 'The Countess Cathleen', *Collected Plays* (Macmillan, London, 1934).
3 *Domesday Book, 2-Sussex*, text and translation edited by John Morris (Phillimore, Chichester, 1976).
4 John Burroughs, *Winter Sunshine*.
5 Rev. Arthur Young, *A General View of the Agriculture of Sussex*.
6 Maude Robinson, *A South Down Farm in the Sixties*. [1860s]
7 W. H. Hudson, *A Shepherd's Life*.
8 Maude Robinson, op. cit.
9 Old Sussex song.
10 Thomas Hardy, *Far From the Madding Crowd* (Macmillan, London, 1902).
11 W. H. Hudson, 'Chichester', in *Nature in Downland*.

Chapter 6

1 Edward Thomas, 'October', in *Collected Poems* (Faber, London, 1974).
2 Richard Jefferies, *The Story of My Heart* (Longmans Green, London, 1883).
3 See Richard Mabey, *The Common Ground*.
4 John Steinbeck, *Travels with Charley in Search of America*, quoted in Shoard, op. cit.
5 Massingham, op. cit.
6 For an account of the reserve and its wildlife, see Richard Williams, *The Great Yew Forest* (Macmillan, London, 1978).
7 The headquarters for England of the Nature Conservancy Council are at Calthorpe House, Calthorpe Street, Banbury, Oxfordshire, OX16 8EX. Other reserves are managed by local trusts, councils, and

bodies such as the National Trust. Many nature reserves are open to the public, or may be walked through along public footpaths. For others, permission to visit is needed, from regional officers or local wardens. Of particular interest in downland are: the Wye and Crundale Downs, Kent (National Nature Reserve) – wood and grassland typical of the North Downs, with many species of rare orchid; Castle Hill, Sussex (NNR); Mount Caburn, Sussex – noted for chalk-hill blues on its south-facing scarp; Lullington Heath, Sussex (NNR) – the best remaining example of chalk heath, where acid-loving plants (heather, common tormentil) can combine with chalk plants (salad burnet, dropwort) on land where sandy soil overlies the chalk so that the acid/alkalinity balance of the topsoil is near neutral; Box Hill – famous for chalk flora, but also for chalk heath and scrub, box and juniper; White Downs, Surrey – the best juniper site remaining on the North Downs; Compton Down, Isle of Wight – known for its butterflies, and as the best example of chalk downland influenced by maritime conditions; Martin Down, Hants (NNR) – grazed by local landowners, outstanding for butterflies (silver-spotted skipper, Adonis blue), with roe deer, brown hare, adders, birds such as hen harriers (in winter), hobbies, and occasionally Montagu's harrier; Eggardon, Hod and Hambledon Hills in Dorset; Aston Upthorpe Down, Berks; Pewsey Downs, Wilts; Old Winchester Hill (NNR) – grazed and ungrazed grassland, flowers such as rampion and autumn gentian, butterflies and birds of prey; along the valleys of the Wylye and Ebble, blocks of downland that are outstanding as grassland, probably one of the oldest grasslands in England, rich in flowers – Wylye Down (NNR), Prescombe Down (NNR); Parsonage Down (unploughed for centuries in parts), with others in that region. Porton Down, Wilts, owned by the Ministry of Defence, and therefore not open to the public, is probably the largest continuous area of chalk downland left in England, but has fewer rare plants because it has been ploughed in the past.

8 Massingham, op. cit.
9 John Aubrey, *The Natural History of Wiltshire*.
10 John Aubrey, *The Natural History and Antiquities of the County of Surrey*.
11 Richard Jefferies, *The Story of My Heart*.
12 Richard Jefferies, 'Out of Doors in February', in *The Open Air*.
13 Two quotes from Richard Jefferies, *The Story of My Heart*.
14 From *The Book of the Open Air*, edited by Edward Thomas.
15 John Burroughs, *Winter Sunshine*.

Chapter 7

1 Letter to Lord Alfred Douglas, July–August 1894. *The Letters of Oscar Wilde*, edited by Rupert Hart-Davis (Hart-Davis, London, 1962).
2 Letter to Charles Spurrier Mason, August 1894. Ibid.
3 Letter to George Alexander. Ibid.
4 Letter to Flaxman, 21 September 1800. *The Letters of William Blake*, edited by Geoffrey Keynes (Hart-Davis, London, 1956).
5 Letter to Thomas Butts, 23 September 1800. Ibid.
6 Letter to George Richmond, October 1834, *The Life and Letters of Samuel Palmer* (Seeley & Co, London, 1892).
7 Letter to John Linnell. Quoted in David Cecil, *Visionary and Dreamer*.
8 David Cecil, op. cit.
9 Letter from Rottingdean, 1883. In Georgiana Burne-Jones, *Memorials of Edward Burne-Jones*.
10 In 1887 when he was 55. Op. cit.
11 From Hilaire Belloc, 'Ha'nacker Mill', in *Complete Verse* (Duckworth, London, 1970).
12 From Hilaire Belloc, 'Fragmentary Prelude', in *Complete Verse*.
13 Shelley, 'On Love', *The Prose Works of Shelley* (Chatto & Windus, London, 1888).
14 Shelley, 'Song'. Published by Mrs Shelley, *Posthumous Poems* (1824).
15 Ted Walker, *The High Path* (Routledge & Kegan Paul, London, 1982).
16 Letter to Richard Wordsworth, 19 March 1797. In E. de Selincourt, *Dorothy Wordsworth – A Biography*.
17 Letter to Jane Marshall, 30 November 1795. Ibid.

18· Journal, 26 January 1798. In *The Journals of Dorothy Wordsworth*, edited by E. de Selincourt (Macmillan, London, 1941).
19 Letter to William Mathews, 21 March 1796, *Early Letters of William and Dorothy Wordsworth* (Clarendon Press, Oxford, 1935).
20 John Betjeman, 'Dorset', in *Collected Poems* (Murray, London, 1958).
21 Letter to Edith Shackleton Heald, 15 March 1938. In *The Letters of W. B. Yeats*, edited by Allan Wade (Hart-Davis, London, 1954).
22 Letter to George and Georgiana Keats, 14 February 1819, op. cit.
23 John Ruskin, 'Dilecta', in *Praeterita* (Allen, Orpington, 1885–1900).
24 Letter to Alice Stuart-Wortley, 1924.
25 Thomas Hardy, *Under the Greenwood Tree* (Macmillan, London, 1903).
26 Thomas Hardy, *The Return of the Native*. The area is threatened further by being shortlisted as a site for a vast nuclear power station complex, with towers 400 or 540 feet high, visible 30 to 40 miles away – probably the largest man-made structure in southern England.
27 D. H. Lawrence, *England My England* (Thomas Seltzer, New York, 1922).
28 Virginia Woolf, op. cit.
29 Helen Thomas, introduction to Edward Thomas, *The South Country*.
30 All the above quotations are from Edward Thomas, *The South Country*.
31 From 'Roads', in Edward Thomas, *Collected Poems*.

Chapter 8
1 John Fowles, *The Enigma of Stonehenge*. © 1980 by the Philpot Museum.
2 Aubrey Burl, op. cit.
3 John Fowles, op. cit.
4 Old ballad.
5 Kipling, 'Sussex', from 'The Five Nations', *Collected Poems* (Methuen, London, 1908).
6 John Burroughs, *Winter Sunshine*.
7 Philip Gosse, *Go to the Country* (Cassell, London, 1935).
8 Samuel J. Looker, *Shelley, Trelawny and Henley*.
9 See Catherine Dupré, *John Galsworthy*. Rudolf Sauter, quoted in H. V. Marrot, *The Life and Letters of John Galsworthy* (Heinemann, London, 1935). The lines 'high to the cool sky' and following lines are from Galsworthy's well-known poem.
10 Account by R. H. Sauter. The poem 'Scatter My Ashes' was found by Galsworthy's family after his death – 'to go with my Will'.
11 Richard Jefferies, *The Story of My Heart*. Near Barbury hillfort, which Jefferies loved to visit, is an inscription from the same book, the quotation at the end of this chapter.
12 Thomas Hardy, 'Wessex Heights', in *Collected Poems*.

Bibliography

The works of Richard Jefferies, W. H. Hudson and Edward Thomas are increasingly available in paperback, but some are available in the original editions only. (*Jefferies' Countryside*, edited by Samuel J. Looker, Constable, 1944, contains essays and a complete summary of Jefferies's writings.) Particular works by these authors are referred to in the notes.

Anderson, J. R. L., and Godwin, Fay, *The Oldest Road* (Wildwood House, 1975).
Arkell, T. Reginald, *Richard Jefferies* (Rich and Cowan, 1933).
Atkinson, R. J. C., *Stonehenge and Neighbouring Monuments* (HMSO, London, 1978).
Aubrey, John, *The Natural History of Wiltshire*, 1847. (Reprint edition, David & Charles, Newton Abbot, 1969).
____, *The Natural History and Antiquities of the County of Surrey* (London, 1719).
Belloc, Hilaire, *The Old Road* (Constable, London, 1904).
Brome, James, *Travels Over England, Scotland and Wales* (London, 1700).
Burl, Aubrey, *Prehistoric Avebury* (Yale University Press, New Haven and London, 1979).
Burne-Jones, Edward, *The Flower Book – Reproductions of Thirty-Eight Watercolour Designs* (Fine Art Society, 1905).
Burne-Jones, Georgiana, *Memorials of Edward Burne-Jones* (Macmillan, London, 1904).
Burroughs, John, *Winter Sunshine* (David Douglas, Edinburgh, 1883).
Butlin, Martin, *William Blake* (Tate Gallery, London, 1978).
Cecil, David, *Visionary and Dreamer* (Constable, London, 1962).
Cheetham, J. H., and Piper, John, *Wiltshire* (Shell Guide), (Faber, London, 1968).
Cobbert, William, *Rural Rides* (Dent Everyman's Library, London, 1966–7).
Curwen, E. Cecil, *Sussex*, (Country Archaeologies) (Methuen, London, 1937).
Darby, Ben, *The South Downs* (Hale, London, 1976).
Dupré, Catherine, *John Galsworthy* (Collins, London, 1976).
Dutton, Ralph, *The English Country House* (Batsford, London, 1935).
Dyer, James, *Southern England: An Archaeological Guide* (Faber, London, 1973).
Erredge, John Ackerson, *History of Brighthelmston* (Brighton, 1862).
Ford, John H., *Sussex* (Alfred Knopf, 1929).
Fowles, John and Brukoff, Barry, *The Enigma of Stonehenge* (Cape, London, 1980).
Fraser, John Lloyd, *John Constable* (Hutchinson, London, 1976).
Garner, H., *Modern British Farming Systems* (Elek, London, 1972).
Girouard, Mark, *Life in the English Country House* (Yale University Press, New Haven and London, 1978).
Gittings, Robert, *Young Thomas Hardy* (Heinemann, London, 1975).
____, *The Older Hardy* (Heinemann, London, 1978).
Hardy, Florence Emily, *The Life of Thomas Hardy* (Macmillan, London, 1962).
Harrison, David, *Along the South Downs* (Cassell, London, 1958).
Hawkins, Desmond, *Cranborne Chase* (Gollancz, London, 1980).

Hughes, A. M. D., *The Nascent Mind of Shelley* (Clarendon Press, Oxford, 1947).
Hunn, David, *Goodwood* (Davis-Poynter, 1975).
Jenkins, Herbert, *William Blake* (Herbert Jenkins, 1925).
Jennet, Seán, *South Downs Way* (HMSO, London, 1977).
Jones, Frederick L. (ed.), *The Letters of Percy Bysshe Shelley* (OUP, Oxford, 1964).
Jones, Sydney R., *English Village Homes* (Batsford, London, 1936).
Kent, John, *Records and Reminiscences of Goodwood and the Dukes of Richmond* (London, 1896).
Le Borne, *Récits d'une Tante – Mémoires de la Comtesse de Boigne* (Paris, 1907).
Looker, Samuel J., *Shelley, Trelawny and Henley* (Worthing, 1950).
Mabey, Richard, *The Common Ground* (Hutchinson in assoc. with NCC, London, 1980).
Marshall, John, *Sussex Cricket – A History* (Heinemann, London, 1959).
Massingham, H. J., *English Downland* (Batsford, London, 1936).
Meade-Fetherstonhaugh, Margaret and Warner, Oliver, *Uppark and Its People* (Allen & Unwin, London, 1964).
Musgrave, Clifford, *Life in Brighton* (Faber, London, 1970).
Pitt, Derek, and Shaw, Michael, *Surrey Villages* (Hale, London, 1971).
Purdy, Richard Little, and Millgate, Michael, *The Collected Letters of Thomas Hardy* (Clarendon Press, Oxford, 1978).
Pyatt, Edward C., *Chalkways of South and South-East England* (David & Charles, Newton Abbot, 1974).
Reeves, H. L., *Adur to Arun* (Sheepdown Publications, Findon, 1970).
Robinson, Maude, *A South Down Farm in the Sixties* (Dent, London, 1938).
Selincourt, Basil de, *William Blake* (Duckworth, London, 1909).
Selincourt, Ernest de, *Dorothy Wordsworth. A Biography* (Clarendon Press, Oxford, 1933).
Shepherd, Walter, *Flint* (Faber, London, 1972).
Shoard, Marion, *The Theft of the Countryside* (Temple Smith, London, 1980).
Shrubb, Michael, *The Birds of Sussex* (Phillimore, Chichester, 1979).
Sitwell, Osbert, and Barton, Margaret, *Brighton* (Faber, London, 1935).
Street, Pamela, *Portrait of Wiltshire* (Hale, London, 1971).
Taylor Christopher, *Dorset* (Hodder & Stoughton, London, 1970).
———, *Roads and Tracks of Britain* (Dent, London, 1979).
Thomas, Edward, *A Literary Pilgrim in England* (Cape, London, 1917).
———, (ed.), *The Book of the Open Air* (Hodder & Stoughton, London, 1907).
———, *The South Country* (Dent, London, 1932).
Timperley, H. W., and Brill, Edith, *Ancient Trackways of Wessex* (Phoenix House, 1965).
White, Gilbert, *The Natural History of Selborne* (1788–9). (Penguin, Harmondsworth, 1977).
Wright, Christopher John, *A Guide to the Pilgrim's Way and North Downs Way* (Constable, London, 1971).
Wright, Geoffrey N., *View of Wessex* (Hale, London, 1978).
Wymer, Norman, *Companion into Sussex* (Methuen, London, 1950).
Young, Rev. Arthur, *A General View of the Agriculture of Sussex* (London, 1808).

Index